D1265618

As I Remember Fordham

AS I REMEMBER FORDHAM

*Selections
from the
Sesquicentennial
Oral History Project*

The Office of the Sesquicentennial
FORDHAM UNIVERSITY
1991

Copyright © 1991 by FORDHAM UNIVERSITY
All rights reserved.
LC 91–61628
ISBN 0–8232–1338–2
Printed in the United States of America

Distributed by Fordham University Press

This book is dedicated
to
the Faculty of Fordham
1841–1991
the men and women
whose learning has opened the minds
and
whose lives have inspired the hearts
of our students
these one hundred fifty years

CONTENTS

A MESSAGE FROM THE PRESIDENT

A UNIVERSITY, like any great institution, transcends the experience of any single generation. At the same time, the people who make up the university community shape the meaning of its tradition and give it heart and voice.

Through this Oral History Project, many of the men and women who played important roles in Fordham's history express their own memories of the University. Each adds a special angle of vision on the many-sided life of Fordham. Their words, captured in living testimony and recorded in these excerpts, keep the sense of Fordham's past alive and help us translate that past into a promise for the future.

I want to congratulate all those who have contributed to this project but most especially Rev. Joseph R. Frese, s.j., who was the founding Chairman of the Oral History Project, and Mrs. Stella Moundas, the Coordinator of the Sesquicentennial, who has shepherded this project from start to finish with her customary care and great love for Fordham.

JOSEPH A. O'HARE, S.J.

EDITOR'S NOTE

I FIRST SAW FORDHAM in September 1967, and as I wrote in *Fordham* magazine almost twenty years later:

I thought my 12-year-old heart would never mend. My brother, Tim, who doubled as my best friend, was going off to college. The only thing I knew about the place called "Rose Hill" and the people called "Jesuits" was that they were taking my brother away from Geneva, New York, and the big, red brick house that six kids and their parents called home.

My heart did mend and my affection for Fordham grew, so much that I followed my brother to the Bronx six years later. When I graduated from Fordham College in May 1977, I was proud to be a part of the grand tradition of Fordham.

My pride is much greater today because my knowledge and understanding of Fordham and its people are much deeper. As the editor of this volume of excerpts from the Sesquicentennial Oral History Project, I have had the unusual privilege of reading the recollections of 75 of Fordham's dedicated teachers and administrators and loyal alumni. Their words have brought to life individuals, academic departments, pivotal events, even buildings from days gone by and from venues as varied as Rose Hill, the Woolworth Building, 302 Broadway, Lincoln Center, and Tarrytown. Collectively, they offer answers to questions that all of us seek, whether we are perusing the morning newspaper or studying an historian's text: who, when, and what, but also how and why.

The excerpts contained in this volume are not intended to be a complete history of the University or any of its individual colleges and schools. And they represent, of course, only a portion of each participant's lengthier recollections, which are available in the University Archives. I hope you will see them as I do, almost as letters from friends, acquaintances, or strangers, letters which may prompt a knowing smile or perhaps a forgotten tear, but which at the very least offer a glimpse of Fordham's proud history from those who have lived it and, in many cases, shaped it.

JERRY BUCKLEY
Fordham College
Class of 1977

INTRODUCTION

ON NOVEMBER 16, 1987, at a luncheon for professors emeriti, Rev. Joseph A. O'Hare, S.J., President of Fordham University, announced the establishment of the Professors Emeriti Oral History Project. Initiated as a means to record the history of Fordham through the memories of its retired faculty, the Project (renamed the Oral History Project to reflect the broadened scope of its coverage) has grown to encompass a larger area of the University experience. It now involves a wide range of administration, faculty, alumni, and staff, including (at the urging of John D. Feerick, Dean of the School of Law) a selection of Fordham's law graduates, many of whom have held substantial positions in both government and the private sector.

Compiling a history of any institution on the eve of its sesquicentennial is a difficult task since, in the attempt accurately to record the quickly receding distant past, the recent past may be neglected. Mindful of this challenge, the Oral History Project has attempted to include among its interviewees those with memories of many years ago as well as those with more contemporary recollections. This volume contains excerpts from the first 75—of a total 150—interviews the Project completed. The order in which the excerpts are presented here is alphabetical, except for those of the three former Presidents; theirs are presented first, and in the chronological sequence of their terms. Leo McLaughlin, President of the University from 1965 to 1969, was invited to do an interview for the Project, but his health would not permit him to participate.

The Fordham Oral History Project is intended to provide an historical account based upon taped and transcribed oral recollections. Researchers may either listen to an interview or read the interview transcript. After an interview was completed, the tape was copied and transcribed verbatim; the transcript was then submitted to the interviewee for editing. When the corrected transcript was returned and the corrections incorporated into a final transcript, two copies were made on archival-quality, non-acidic paper, and bound. Since the transcripts have been edited by the participants, there is not an exact correspondence between the tape and the transcript. After the Sesquicentennial, the holdings of the Project will be deposited in the University Archives and in the University Libraries for future scholarly use.

Grateful acknowledgment is made to the following persons for their contributions to the development of the Oral History Project: Rev.

Joseph A. O'Hare, s.j., President of Fordham University; Rev. Eugene J. O'Brien, s.j., Chairman of the Sesquicentennial Celebration; William Spencer Reilly, Executive Director of the Sesquicentennial Celebration; John D. Feerick, Dean of the School of Law; Rev. Joseph R. Frese, s.j., founding Chairman of the Oral History Project; Michael Sheahan, University Secretary, whose advice has been invaluable throughout; Harvey Humphrey, Director of the Media Center at Rose Hill; the many volunteers who conducted interviews for the Project, especially Robert H. Cooper, Jr., and Clement London; Christopher L. Constas, who gave long and dedicated service to the project as a graduate assistant; and, of course, those men and women who were gracious enough to grant us interviews.

STELLA MOUNDAS
Coordinator
Oral History Project

REV. LAURENCE J. McGINLEY, S.J.

Rev. Laurence J. McGinley, S.J., was President of Fordham from 1949 to 1963.

The Genesis of Fordham at Lincoln Center

Father Gannon bought a building, called the Vincent Building, which was at Duane Street and Broadway. That was the place that downtown Fordham went from the Woolworth Building. It contained the School of Education, the School of Law, and the downtown Business School. As the three schools prospered, there were classes going from very early in the morning to late at night. It was obvious to me, shortly after I got to Fordham in 1949, that we had to do something to get more room. The purpose of having a downtown

school at all was to facilitate professional people to attend Fordham instead of having to come the considerable distance to Rose Hill.

We had a meeting in the fall of 1955 of the real estate advisory committee I had formed. George Hammer came with a new proposal. "Do you know Bob Moses?" he asked me. I said, "Yes, I do." He said, "Do you have entrée to him?" I said, "Yes, I do" because he knew my Dad and liked me, and when I came to New York, he sort of adopted me as somebody he's known in the cradle.

George said, "Go to see him and ask him if you can rent five floors in the Coliseum Building (which was being built at the time). Tell him it's about the size you need and ask him if you could also have the right to use the big Coliseum itself for major events of the University. Bob will turn that down. If he does agree to it, fine, but I don't think he will. I think what he will do is say 'why don't you let me bring you in on the Urban Development Program at 9th Avenue and 59th Street.' "

I made an appointment to see Bob Moses and went out to Babylon, Long Island, to see him. He was very gracious, and I was kind of scared and I gave my story. "No, you don't want that," he said. "It's not built for that purpose. It's built for offices. In schools everybody moves at the

1

end of the class hour. They all use elevators. Why don't you let me bring you in on the urban renewal project a block west of that?"

So I said, "What is an urban renewal project?" and I got it explained to me all over again, more or less. So he said, "Let's see. How much room would you need? Ten acres?" I almost fell off my chair. I was thinking about something about twice the size of the Vincent Building. When he mentioned acres I couldn't believe it. I never heard anyone talk about New York City real estate in terms of acres. I gulped. He had a map of streets and he said, "Look, maybe a couple of these blocks; that would be about ten acres or something like that."

In those days we had plenty of superiors—a Provincial, a General, and the Cardinal, and everybody was in the act. I went back and told the Provincial about the possibility, and he suggested I clear it with the Cardinal first thing. So I went down and saw Cardinal Spellman and he said, "This is the greatest thing that has happened to Fordham since my predecessor Archbishop Hughes built the University up at Rose Hill." So there was no flack there.

It was called Lincoln Square Urban Renewal. We were the first to accept specifically, and I picked the southeast corner of the five-block project. I did it for two reasons. It was nearest to the central subway system at Lincoln Center. And I wanted to be right across from St. Paul's Church. Sentimentally, I wanted that because that was where my mother had gone when she was a young woman and my uncle had done some of the architectural work there. The practical reason was because I felt we would not need to build a big church that could hold our students as a group.

We had to overcome some legal obstacles. There was a lawyer who was a crusader against urban renewal. He didn't believe in it. He thought it was unfair to move people out of their little happy homes. Actually they weren't. They were ghetto homes, and it was not a happy place. But he got publicity, of course, and reporters asked him, "What are you going to do?" He said, "I am going to bring up the church–state issue. Fordham is part of this and it is the easiest issue to bring up and that will stop it."

I talked it over with Bill O'Shea, who was the University attorney at the time, and decided that I wanted to fight it and that I was going to pick the ground on which to fight it. The one ground offered was that we really weren't a Catholic institution. There were a lot of legal reasons to prove that but I refused. I did not want to fight it on the grounds that we could claim we were not Catholic. I fought it on the grounds that whoever we were this was a bona fide project of the government and that any person who qualifies under the terms of the project should be able to buy land. The suit never actually caused things to come to a full halt but we went all the way to the U.S. Supreme Court twice, first through the state courts and then through the federal courts and we won every single time all the way up.

We decided to build the Law School first—that was all the money we had to build. The rest [of Fordham] was in the works when I left Fordham. Somewhere along the line a petition was sent to John Rockefeller, a member of the project's board of directors, asking if Fordham could call itself "Fordham at Lincoln Center." The board said, as a tribute to me, they would be delighted to do so. It was important because they sued anyone immediately who used the Lincoln Center name on anything because it was a patented trademark for the performing arts complex.

Some people have asked, "Why didn't Columbia do this project?" Well, they didn't ask. I guess that is the simplest way to put it. I asked. I asked Bob Moses, "What should I do?"

REV. VINCENT T. O'KEEFE, S.J.

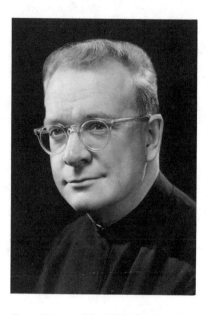

Rev. Vincent T. O'Keefe joined the Society of Jesus in 1937. He came to Fordham in 1960 as Academic Vice President and two years later was appointed the University's first Executive Vice President. In 1963 he was appointed as Fordham's 27th President. In the summer of 1965, following a General Congregation of the Jesuits in Rome, Father O'Keefe was elected to serve as one of four Assistants to the Father General of the Order, Pedro Arrupe. Father O'Keefe did not return to Fordham until 1984 when he was appointed Rector of the Fordham·Jesuit Community. He is now Superior of the Provincial Residence at Kohlmann Hall on the Rose Hill campus.

On Becoming
Fordham's President

The *Status* was a Jesuit tradition. It was the list that the Provincial would send to each individual Jesuit house noting the changes in positions the individual Jesuits would have. It was released on a day in June that frequently coincided with the Feast of the Sacred Heart. (I guess that added to your motivation.) It would be posted on the main bulletin board of the Jesuit community and for most people that was the first they heard of where they were being sent. I was on my way to my old quarters at Woodstock in Maryland to make my annual retreat and the Provincial, John McGinty, asked me to stop and see him. He told me, "I hope you make a good retreat because when you come back I want to announce that I'm going to make you President of Fordham University."

On Starting Thomas
More College

We had done a lot of soundings, especially around the metropolitan area, and we didn't want to impose any further difficulty on the Catholic women's colleges, but we did find a real desire on the part of a lot of young women to go to a university where you had all the obvious advantages a university can provide and also to share in mixed company with the young gentlemen.

Well, Fordham College wouldn't hear of this. Fordham College was a male precinct, as it were, and there was no idea of introducing young ladies there. In the eyes of many people, especially the Jesuits, Fordham University really was Fordham College. We said, let's try it this way. Thomas More started in 1964, and the first two years we really had a mix of extraordinary students who proved every bit as intelligent and productive as the young men, and I think they had a good influence on the men. It wasn't like soothing the savage beast or anything like that, but it was a good influence.

Father John Donohue, one of our favorites, was the first Dean and he explained why they called it Thomas More College. He said that Thomas More had gone to great troubles to educate his daughters and that he emphasized the liberal arts and was a great model for the Christian gentleman. The students were excellent so that after a time the fears about Fordham College were allayed and eventually the two schools merged into the coeducational Fordham College.

On the Creation of the Faculty Senate

During the course of a self-study in the mid-1960s, it came out that really the voice of the faculty, as a group, in not setting but at least having an input into University policy was very limited. Also, we wanted it to be the Fordham faculty, not the Jesuit faculty. So we decided we should do what many other universities had already done and set up an honest-to-goodness faculty senate which would be an elected body and would help the general administration in setting policy.

Our dear friend Joseph Cammarosano was elected the first president and he got them off to a great start. It still goes today. It is, I think, after the novelty wears off, a very tiresome thing—they put in long hours. But I think it has proven a betterment. You are always going to have conflicts between faculty and administration. But at least now there is a structured way for having the faculty, who after all do the teaching and have the closest contact with the students, participate and have their views heard on different policies, like the different standards for admission, the curriculum, faculty salaries and then that prime question—parking space.

On Why a Speech by George Wallace Was Called Off

A student who was a member of the American Age lecture series had been traveling during the summer of 1964 and he stopped in Alabama and met with George Wallace's people. Wallace at that time was intending to run for President in 1964 and this student said to Wallace's advisers, "How would you like to speak in New York City and get a New York platform?" When he came back to campus he was almost sick with concern. What had developed in the meantime was that terrible bombing and fire in the church in Birmingham, Alabama, in which several people were killed. Wallace would have appeared at Fordham in the American Age series not even a week after that terrible tragedy. The local police called and said if he comes to campus we'll need every policeman in New York City. I thought since this would have represented a great risk to the whole community, I called it off, for which we were sacked in the press. If I had to do it again today, I would do the same thing.

REV. JAMES C. FINLAY, S.J.

Rev. James C. Finlay, S.J., a 1944 graduate of Fordham College, was Instructor of Political Science from 1960 to 1968, Dean of the Graduate School of Arts and Sciences from 1968 to 1972, and President of the University from 1972 to 1984.

". . . I am very emotional in my attachment to Fordham. To Fordham I owe whatever I have accomplished over the years, and I love this University now even more than I did years ago."

The above statement may seem surprising, coming as it does from one who never sought the presidency of Fordham and who did his best to decline it when the offer came. It does, however, help explain the steady attention and dedication James Finlay gave to that responsibility during one of the longest presidential tenures in Fordham's history.

Future historians of the University should have no trouble identifying the central thrust of the Finlay years. Almost from the start, it became clear that Finlay believed that if Fordham was to maintain and improve its position as a responsible, responsive component of American higher education, there must be new initiatives taken on a number of fronts both within and without the University. Many of these he started himself; others he supported heartily. At the close of his administration he had kept Fordham enrollment high, approved expenditures for a steadily improving physical plant, encouraged efforts to achieve a wider geographical mix of students, and presided over an impressive string of consecutively balanced budgets that provided an essential base for stimulating new ventures in teaching and research.

He summarizes his fourteen years as President this way:

I doubt that many university presidents experienced a more quiet entry into their new responsibilities than did I. With Fordham still wrestling its way through a difficult financial period in the early '70s, the absence of pomp and ceremony seemed just right to me. I remember driving out to the airport with my distinguished and greatly liked predecessor, Michael Walsh, S.J., who was headed for

Boston and new duties there. Just before boarding his plane, Mike handed me the keys to his car, and that was that. Except for a brief introduction of me during commencement as the next Fordham President, the transfer of an ignition key marked my official entry into my new work and challenges.

Listing just a few of the major undertakings in which I had some involvement gives me the chance to name at least a few of the many colleagues, Jesuits and lay persons, who helped make my years as the University's chief officer so stimulating and rewarding.

I naturally made a number of new administrative appointments, but one of my very best personnel decisions was not an appointment at all. To my good fortune, and Fordham's as well, Dr. Joseph Cammarosano agreed to postpone his deeply felt personal desire to return to teaching and stay on as Executive Vice President. That meant we could continue to rely on his exceptional leadership in restoring Fordham's finances to good health. When this brilliant economist was finally, but reluctantly, released by me so that he could return to his classrooms, another trusted administrator, Dr. Paul Reiss, was prepared by training, temperament, and ability to take over, which he so capably did in the closing years of my administration.

Then there were three successive Chairmen of the Board of Trustees, all sons of Fordham, who labored effectively and generously to make this place a better one. Mr. Felix Larkin, for many years a principal officer of W. R. Grace & Company, led us through a massive and long overdue reorganization of record-keeping, billing procedures, and management of income and endowment funds. Equally valuable help in another form came from Mr. George Doty, the Wall Street financier, and Mr. Richard Bennett, the pharmaceuticals executive. Both George and Dick not only taught a somewhat shy administration how to ask for money, but set the example for many by the quiet, generous contributions of their own.

The work of these men and others helped buttress a conviction of mine that grew ever more strongly over the years—the conviction that there should be much greater participation and sharing in Catholic affairs and enterprises by the laity. Even as Fordham has held fast to the time-tested Jesuit belief that good teaching also incorporates guidance that helps students develop their own styles of good ethical behavior, it has not hesitated in more recent times to welcome Catholic and non-Catholic lay leaders into almost all aspects of University life and governance.

With fiscal problems fast coming under control, we were able to address other important matters, and for me one of these had to be the Bronx, where Fordham roots lie deep. I was dismayed by the environmental and human aspects of decay outside the perimeter of Rose Hill, and I admit that one of my first acts to address a nearby problem had more vigor than intellect behind it. To city officials who would listen and to those who would not, I insisted more often than either group liked that a once-viable building across Fordham Road from the Third Avenue gate must be demolished to rid the area of a dangerous, disreputable eyesore. From that humble beginning we ventured into more important catalyst roles that stressed better neighborhood housing for the elderly and disabled, new entrepreneurial starts, neighborhood coalition formations to press for legitimate political action and response, and similar actions. I gladly note that some of Fordham's best young students, graduate and undergraduate, put time and talent to this demanding extracurricular work. Father Paul Brant (now chaplain at St. Peter's College in Jersey City) and Dr. Brian Byrne (now Vice President for Administration) are representative of many others who have my gratitude and respect. Father Brant who, at the time was a teaching assistant in the Philosophy Department, became the driving force behind the development of the North West Bronx Clergy Coalition, which still provides leadership in the local communities. Dr. Byrne became a volunteer with the Coalition

while still a graduate student. Subsequently, I chose him to be my right-hand man for community affairs, and Father O'Hare later promoted him to his current position. The senior staff of the Coalition, now a multi-million-dollar enterprise, includes several individuals who began their work there as undergraduates.

One reason that I encouraged and listened to many new ideas for teaching effectiveness from our faculty stemmed from some of my own student memories of Fordham in the early '40s. There were brilliant intellects on campus then as now, but I also recall a lot of inferior teaching whose tempo never changed from year to year. To those who sometimes remind me of "those good old days," I sometimes reply. "Well, number one, I remember them too so they can't be that old. And, second, they weren't so good because I experienced them." These are opinions that probably will not please everybody, but I am convinced that the quality of teaching at the Lincoln Center and Rose Hill campuses is now better and more constant than much of the instruction I received as an undergraduate. Some of the most enthusiastic opinions about Fordham teaching have come from the Presidential and Jesuit Community scholars we enrolled at Fordham as a worthy reward for their high school scholastic achievements. I am very proud of my fellow Jesuits and, indeed, all our faculty for their welcome to these gifted young people.

A word about Fordham's physical appearance. We all felt good that the new Lombardi Center's completion coincided nicely with the impulse to achieve good physical fitness that swept across our campus and the nation in the '70s. Timely as that fine building was, however, other needs seemed even more pressing, in particular the renovation and renewal of physical plant at Rose Hill. We all gulped at the estimated price tag for this effort—something like $24 million, I recall—but then we gulped again and began rebuilding walls, repointing stone and brick, replacing ancient, unsafe electrical systems, and transforming essentially sound and attractive but outdated buildings into comfortable dormitories. Neither I nor my colleagues care particularly to be remembered as a "caretaker administration," but refurbishing, remodeling, and better caretaking were overdue, and Rose Hill is much the better for it all. The Lincoln Center campus, thank goodness, did not yet need such investment, but it is also getting its fair share of updating in this decade. The addition to the Law School, honoring alumnus Ned Doyle, was one of the last achievements of the Finlay era.

Alumni as well as students seemed to appreciate these improvements, and said so when they returned to campus in increasing numbers, thanks particularly to programs arranged by the energetic Ralph DeMayo, Director of Alumni Relations, and his staff. The summer alumni reunions particularly were joyous days, and they were also great times for me to meet informally with attendees and their families. Along with their opinions about how Fordham was being managed came a steadily increasing number of pledged gifts from all parts of the country.

At this point I almost regret attempting this summary, for where is the space I really need to acknowledge so much inspired and often selfless service from so many? No adequate summary can be given of such achievements as the establishment of the Graduate School of Religion and Religious Education administered by exactly the right individual for its beginning years, Vincent Novak, s.j. There were those who set up the auxiliary campus at Tarrytown, New York. Professor James Kurtz combined student choirs to send glorious sound through the University Church and across the Rose Hill campus at Christmas. Dr. Lloyd Rogler, our Albert Schweitzer Chair professor, wisely directed its influence into furthering Hispanic studies. There were some astonishingly inspired moments of theater at Lincoln Center directed by Dr. David Davis. Nor is there space to acknowledge the resolution of larger issues that are inevitable companions in university governance—such as the delicate matter of merging Thomas More College with Fordham College in a fair and equitable way, and the 1973 faculty vote to limit tenure that had passionate champions on both sides of the issue.

Future historians of Fordham will give a deeper and far more balanced overview of matters in which I was involved than I can hope to do here. I will accept their appraisals willingly if they will but grant me one small favor. Somewhere in their texts, I hope they will indicate that while other Presidents may have accomplished more, no President could have ever cared more deeply for Fordham than I.

ROBERT ADAMSON

Dr. Robert Adamson, a former senior editor at Cambridge University Press in New York, was the founding director of The College at Sixty at Lincoln Center in 1973. He served as director until 1984.

The College at Sixty

One day, in the middle of January 1973, Dean Shea approached me after lunch in the faculty cafeteria and said he was now ready to add the third stage to his Liberal Arts College (LAC) and would I care to join him in his office to explore how it might be adapted to Fordham's mid-Manhattan campus, obviously non-residential.

He had won a long struggle to unite under one umbrella two undergraduate programs: LAC, a daytime college for traditional students, 18–22; and EXCEL, an evening "General Studies" college for career or household-age young adults. He liked the idea of adding a third stage since, as an educator and classical scholar, he agreed with the assumption that the "Plato Academy," or liberal arts, dimension of Western universities was not for youth only. Our goal was to help older adults exercise their intellects.

After our introductory talk, Dean Shea and I met several more times in January to discuss and to reach agreement on essentials. We then began the design of a College at Sixty model that could win the approval of Fordham's administration in the Bronx and also be self-financing. The five pillars on which the third stage was to be built surfaced: (1) Socratic seminars, (2) retirement-age students, (3) Fordham-employed faculty, (4) a CAS administration partially separate and under the authority of Dean Shea, and (5) an Outreach Program to the community.

June 5, 1973, was the "birth" of The College at Sixty. With blueprints and brochures in hand, we traveled to the Bronx to meet representatives of the President and Trustees. Dr. Joseph Cammarosano, Executive Vice President, welcomed us and praised the blueprint, with which he seemed already acquainted. With his economist eye, he noted that unless the program did finance itself from tuition we had agreed to let it go.

Dr. Paul Reiss, Academic Vice President, approved our pilot seminar plans but said he found difficulty with our intention to tell college graduates that they might accumulate credit toward an M.A. degree by taking courses at the College at Lincoln Center. Those undergraduate courses would be unacceptable to the New York State Board of Regents. Fordham had no Graduate School of Arts and Sciences at the Lincoln Center campus to upgrade them.

Except for the M.A. ruling, the day was unclouded. Dr. Cammarosano gave our "constitution" Fordham's approval and his personal blessing in spite of residual doubts that senior citizens on fixed incomes would pay enough to be our sole source of financing. If we had had a bottle of wine, we would have toasted Dr. Cammarosano, the midwife for our "new baby." But many, in diverse ways, have found occasion to do so since.

At 10:30 Thursday morning, October 18, 1973, eleven women and four men assembled in one of the pleasant, well-lighted Fordham classrooms overlooking the Law School and Lincoln Center. The fifteenth person was Professor Irving Cheyette, recently retired as Professor of Music and Education at the State University of New York at Buffalo. He had just moved back to New York City with his wife and was living two or three blocks from Lincoln Center.

On that morning, the 15 of us sat in a semi-circle and spent two or three minutes interviewing a neighbor before introducing him or her to the group. I then gave a ten-minute overview to explain the purpose of our "Major Philosophies" seminar and why thoroughly read assignments of about 30 pages each would be our procedure.

Father George McMahon and Dean Shea had arranged that the class could have lunch together in the faculty cafeteria. Here Dr. Cheyette made a hit as he answered questions about his first-hand aquaintance with the Japanese and Chinese. After lunch the group returned to the classroom and continued its interrogation of Dr. Cheyette. The two-hour sessions (mornings or afternoons) preceded or followed by lunch in the faculty cafeteria did become protocol.

Dr. Eva Stadler, sometime head of the Humanities Department, mastered the methods of the Socratic seminar almost perfectly. I took in time her course on "Three European Novels," wrote two papers, and admired her ability to keep every student in the class participating in a common search for the narrator's ideas in our weekly assignment of 100 pages. And she did this without lecturing and without dominating the lively interchange. Her students made the author come alive in the classroom. Everyone took turns, and Eva saw to it that all were heard. The two hours flew by, and no one had time to lie back and daydream.

We began with one seminar in the humanities and then added three from other departments. Rather than keeping just these four and requiring all certificate students to take one of each (adding sections, of course), we chose to offer, from each of the four departments, a variety of seminars provided they did not duplicate courses in the undergraduate college.

The decision to discourage *auditing* (passive listening) was salutary. In the first decade more than 750 retirement-age women and men were introduced or reintroduced to liberal arts studies through the small faculty-moderated seminars that required assigned reading, term papers, and class participation—a happy outcome that confirmed our faith that the university does not exist exclusively to prepare students for commercial careers.

In like manner our faith that senior citizens could pay a just tuition proved well-grounded. Income from the tuition for our two-credit seminars was more than enough to pay all direct costs for administration, promotion, and honoraria for 20 or more teachers annually. In addition, the tuition left funds amounting at times to 70 per cent and even 100 per cent above direct expenses that we, with gratitude, were able to contribute to Fordham for overhead.

MILTON ALEXANDER

Dr. Milton Alexander is Professor Emeritus of Marketing in Fordham's College of Business Administration. He held the W. R. Grace Professorship at CBA from 1976 to 1981. He retired in 1983 after 28 years at Fordham.

The College of Business Administration

The acceptance of business administration as a full-fledged profession by Americans at large and, if only grudgingly at first, by the academic community is of fairly recent vintage—dating back to the post–World War II era. Hence, the College of Business Administration benefited immensely from this newfound public favor, and from certain other political, social, economic, and technological developments.

Those developments included the burgeoning of the American economy, the sharply increased demand for skilled managerial labor with formal collegiate training, and the G. I. Bill of Rights providing for free college education to returning war veterans anxious to acquire practicable skills in an accredited prestige institution. (CBA was one of only three schools acredited by the American Association of Colleges and Schools of Business in Metropolitan New York at that time.)

Other tangible factors favoring the growth of CBA are also noteworthy: a dedicated, concerned faculty always on call; a choice of two locations, one at Rose Hill for those students who preferred a traditional and, I should add, beautiful campus referred to as the "Country Club" by other students; and a second site near City Hall in the heart of the financial market and, for those days, the center of international trade; the prestige Fordham enjoyed, perhaps worldwide, as being in the Ivy League of Catholic universities; and a highly effective, firm, yet never oppressive school administration. A third set of factors is equally important to me, and that is a profound attachment to spiritual and civic virtues and traditions.

In the mid-1950s, as I was informed by the old-timers who hark back to CBA's inception at the Woolworth Building in the

15

1930s, accounting always enjoyed a primacy among the business disciplines or areas of study. Consequently, it invariably had by far the largest number of majors and, I should add, the strongest influence on curricula and related decisions. Deservedly so, most of my colleagues had to concede, because as a definable profession, it had a lead of hundreds of years on the rest of us— be it finance, management, or marketing, or the various tool disciplines, such as statistics, business law, operations research, and, later on, computer science.

As for my own fledgling area of marketing, it came into its own as a profession only after World War II, with the release of pent-up demand which, of course, had been restrained by the nation's and the world's war effort. Entrepreneurial interest in marketing was further fueled by the unprecedented growth of domestic and world markets. As we, on the faculty committees, examined the fruits of our programs, we were quite satisfied but never smug. We were particularly gratified by corporate demand for our accounting majors,

by our students' exceptionally high standing in CPA exams, and by the avid campus recruiting of marketing and finance graduates.

Still, we were never satisfied with our progress, particularly by the mid-1960s when the computer broke through early resistance, and rapidly became the warp and woof of business decision-making and policy implementation. The faculty and administration of CBA were quite frustrated by our inability to respond quickly to this new and momentous development. But at the time we realized that we had little choice but to persevere until we surmounted Fordham's financial crisis in the late 1960s and early 1970s.

Only then were we able to integrate, quickly and effectively, computer science into the entire business program, to enlarge our faculty with computer science expertise, and, what is equally important, to install computers adequate in number and design for CBA students. This inexorable trend to the dominance of computers in business decisions was in full swing in CBA when I retired in 1983.

ANNE ANASTASI

Dr. Anne Anastasi is Professor Emeritus in the Graduate School of Arts and Sciences.

I came to Fordham in September 1947. Before that, I was Chairman of the Psychology Department at Queens College, the newly opened college of the City University of New York, where I had established the department in February 1939. Prior to Queens College, I taught at Barnard College, having joined its faculty immediately after receiving my Columbia Ph.D. in 1930.

Two specific inducements were held out to me by Robert Rock, then Chairman of the Fordham Psychology Department. They were tendered semi-facetiously and were certainly received in that spirit, but they are nevertheless noteworthy. First, Bob handed me a condensed timetable from what was then the New York Central Railroad and is now, after several metamorphoses, MetroNorth. Since he knew about our house on 38th Street, he convinced me that in 18 minutes the train would convey me in comfort practically from door to door.

The second argument was that I would teach only in the Graduate School, which also meant half as many classroom hours per week as were then standard for undergraduate teaching at Fordham, as at most other colleges. The many intrinsic attractions of graduate teaching, together with additional free time for research and writing, were certainly appealing.

At that time, the only liberal arts college at Fordham was exclusively male, in both student population and faculty. In fact, I was told that a female assistant or secretary could not even enter a classroom to put a notice on the blackboarrd if the regular instructor was absent! When I was appointed, I was the fourth female professor on the Rose Hill campus. The other three were Elizabeth Salmon in Philosophy, Ruth Witkus in Biology, and Dorothea McCarthy in our own department.

I was elected Chairman when Fordham adopted the system of regular rotating Chairmanships. I served for the maximum of six years (1968–1974), having been re-elected after my first three-year term. During these years there were problems aplenty! It was a period of maximal student unrest, together with cuts in the University budget and sharp reductions in government grants.

Still, when I was recently asked for my happiest memories of the Fordham experience, I mentioned that very period—when I was department Chairman and problems were popping out all over. But the problems were solvable, without excessive wasted effort, needless paperwork, or rigid bureaucratic procedures. The key was unity in meeting the problems, with wonderful rapport within the department, with our graduate students, and eventually also with our undergraduate majors.

Unlike what happens in many other universities, the clinical program was fully integrated in our department from the start. We have been justly proud of our implementation of the scientist–professional model. Our students are fully trained as psychologists first, and then move gradually into specialties and subspecialties. These qualities have been recognized repeatedly by clinical and hospital supervisors where our students work as interns or as full-fledged clinicians. The credit for this goes predominantly to Marvin Reznikoff, an outstanding scientist, professional, and human being.

Let me cite one small example of our relationship, an example that also tells us something about Marvin as a person. Because of the budget crisis, the salary increments of two of our recently appointed but highly valued faculty members was insufficient for them to want to remain; both were making plans to move elsewhere. When Marvin and I went to the Academic Vice President with this problem, I offered to forgo my normal increment for that year so the amount could be transferred to the two junior members. Marvin whereupon made the same offer. Both of us were in earnest, and the offers were accepted and implemented. It is noteworthy that neither of the two junior beneficiaries was in the clinical program—both were in experimental.

In 1984, the American Psychological Foundation awarded me its gold medal for lifetime achievement. We usually think of that APF medal as a sort of "terminal" award. Consequently, when I received a phone call from the Science Adviser to President Reagan, telling me I was the recipient of a National Medal for Science for 1987, I was so startled that I blurted out, "Oh my, I thought I already had all there was." Whereupon he replied with quick repartee, "Well, this is one you missed, or rather we missed you, and now we are correcting that omission."

ANTHONY N. BARATTA

Anthony N. Baratta, Chairman of the Division of Curriculum and Teaching at Fordham's Graduate School of Education at Lincoln Center since 1982, joined the School's faculty in 1961. He served as Chairman of the Division of Administration and Supervision for 15 years and as Associate Dean for 3 years.

When I first came to Fordham, I was appointed an Assistant Professor of Education and, at that time, the School of Education was mainly an undergraduate program, a very strong liberal arts program, and the Graduate School was a department. I was in the Division of Elementary Education. The Dean of the School was Dr. James Donnelly, who had been a history professor. Dr. Donnelly had followed in the footsteps of the revered Dr. Francis Crowley.

A year after I arrived, Dr. Donnelly left, and he was succeeded by Joseph Probst as an Acting Dean from 1962 to 1965. He was then followed by Dr. Harry Rivlin, who served until 1973. The next person appointed was Dr. Jonathan Messerli, who stayed for four years, and Messerli was succeeded by Dr. Anthony Mottola, who also served for four years. In 1981, Dr. Max Weiner became our dean and is the incumbent.

During my first four years, it was a much more constricted organization than it is today, much more narrowly focused. I don't think we had more than one or two faculty meetings during my first year, and when we did have a meeting, it was a big group because the School then had about 2,000 students and there were faculty members from all the liberal arts and the education programs.

After Dr. Rivlin came and we became a graduate school, he brought a vision of opening up our place. I hate to use the term, but I think we were a more provincial operation in my early years; after the Rivlin years, we garnered a broader vision and at the same time a more focused vision of urban education.

In fact, as a university, given the times and circumstances and our focus on urban education, I think we were ahead of the times. It has not been easy because the focus of urban education is deceptively complex. Within an urban environment, there are so many different types of educational programs, opportunities as well as problems.

How we survived during the difficult periods of the mid-'70s is very interesting. We survived because we have dared to do different things. We expanded to Tarrytown; we went to Puerto Rico and even to Brooklyn. We have a very interesting project in the Bronx right now, and also in East Harlem. We try to adapt.

The Stay in School Program, of which I have been a part, is a good example. It is a cooperative program between Fordham and, for five years, School District 4 in East Harlem and also District 10 in the Bronx. Dean Weiner and Dean Mary Ann Quaranta of the Graduate School of Social Service were instrumental in getting the initial grant from the State Education Department. I have been a co-project manager along with Dr. Theresa Cicchelli from Education and Dr. Pauline Zischka from Social Service.

We try to provide assistance for children from the ages of kindergarten through the fourth grade, children who are considered to be potential dropouts because of an excessive absentee rate. We have provided tutorial and family assistance through case managers, and we have a component in which several of our professors instruct in the program, by working with teachers and parents to look at the educational needs of their children in a more global fashion. The program was expanded to District 10, and we are now in one school in the mid-Bronx.

We were initially one of ten colleges and universities in New York State with the SSPP grant. But only Fordham and the State University of New York at Binghamton are focused on early childhood. We also have one of the few programs that combine the resources of two graduate schools. It is exciting and we're making headway, although the results are never spectacular because it's a slow process.

This kind of program reflects, I think, the culture of Fordham University. I was quite convinced when I came here almost 30 years ago that I had found an institution in which I felt comfortable, could enjoy it, and hopefully could make a contribution with my work. Fordham University has been a superb institution in my opinion.

RICHARD J. BENNETT

Richard J. Bennett was the Chairman of Fordham University's Board of Trustees from 1980 to 1986. A 1938 graduate of Fordham College and a 1942 graduate of Fordham Law School, Mr. Bennett is the retired Chairman of Schering-Plough.

As an undergraduate, I was very active in the Glee Club, which was a very large organization in those days. We had about 80 or 85 young men and we traveled a lot. A Jesuit priest, Father Ted Farley, was the moderator. He had such an influence on all the members of that Club that for years and years after World War II we would all go back to the annual Town Hall Concert of the Glee Club. The Club provided an especially important atmosphere because Fordham was a 99 per cent commuting college in those days.

I was also a member of the Debate Club. I wasn't the top debater or anything, although we did have a couple of really outstanding people. I remember we debated one year against Oxford University and several other universities and Fordham did very well. Even in those early years you realized the value of being able to think on your feet, to articulate, and, above all, to be able to argue both sides of the question.

I was heavily influenced to go to law school, I suppose, by the man I admire to this day the most, my father, who practiced at 14 Wall Street for fifty years. He never pushed me toward law school at all. It was just by example. He made it seem a very rewarding and satisfying career, so by the time I was in my junior year up at Rose Hill, I felt rather strongly that I wanted to follow his steps into law. Ultimately it turned out that my life became quite a different thing from what his was, which is what usually happens.

I found the whole question of studying adequately for the evening law school a very difficult thing, added on to the various other things I was doing. On the other hand, it prepared me in so many ways for my life's work, whatever that work was going to turn out to be, because you really had to discipline yourself very decidedly.

We would pour into the Wool-

21

worth Building, go to class, and then ten o'clock came and we would all take off for our homes. We certainly had to do some studying, and the result was you didn't really get to know intimately your fellow students in the sense that you did during your college days or that you would in a daytime law school where your activities and associations with those other students would be quite manifold.

John Finn and I. Maurice Wormser were outstanding teachers. Totally different types. If you had a predisposition to the law as I had because of my background and my father, they anchored it all down. They made you feel very strongly about it. The fact that they were teaching evening students was an important thing to me about the Law School. It was perfectly obvious that the outstanding professors of the Law School were not only giving their time to the day students, but they were giving it to the evening students too.

They had a tough job because I assume they must have looked out on those bodies in front of them, a lot of them having worked their fannies off that day, some of them married with kids, very young kids obviously, and they must have seen an awful lot of dozing people simply from the sheer inability to keep one's eyes open. But they retained an enormous amount of vitality and spirit about what they were doing. They made you feel it. You were glad you were there, glad you were studying law. I had a great time. I fell asleep a few times myself.

Finn and Wormser were totally different personalities. Wormser spoke more slowly. Some people might have felt he was somewhat thunderous. He was very distinctive. Finn was a very articulate Irishman who discoursed more rapidly. He just had a different way of presenting things.

I was in service on graduation day from the Law School. This was typical of what happened. Because of the war, we were able to take the bar exam in advance of graduation. That's what I did, and I am happy to say that I passed it. It turned out to be a wholly intellectual achievement because when we all came out, everybody was admitted on motion who had graduated from law school.

It was perfectly obvious that one of the reasons I got where I did was that people thought that legally trained people were good people to be decision makers, that they had a way of thinking, a way of deducing answers. I think the law can be a tremendously important background factor. As a matter of fact, one of my predecessors was a lawyer and my successor is a lawyer, so we've had a history of lawyers rising to be CEOs with Schering and Schering-Plough.

CHARLES A. BIRD

Dr. Charles A. Bird is Professor Emeritus in Education and former Associate Dean and Director of Graduate Studies of the School of Education.

My career at Fordham as a faculty member consisted of three phases. Starting in 1950, I worked with seniors in the undergraduate School of Education. Then as an adjunct professor, I taught courses in administration, supervision, and elementary education, in a division supervised by Dr. James Fitzgerald. The third phase was initiated in February 1961 by my appointment as fulltime Associate Professor in the Division of Administration, Supervision, and Secondary Education. This appointment was made by Dr. James Donnelly, then Dean of the School of Education.

In the summer of 1964 Dr. Probst, the Acting Dean of the School of Education, and Father Vincent O'Keefe, s.j., approached me with the suggestion that I consider assuming the position of Director of Graduate Studies. After some soul-searching and discussion, I agreed.

In 1965, Father Mulligan, s.j., Dean of the Graduate School of Arts and Sciences, called a conference of two representatives from the School of Education, one from the History Department and one from the English Department, to consider making an application for a grant to train students in a Master's program providing certification for secondary-school teaching.

As a committee we developed the material for the grant application from the U. S. Department of Education, and I was given the assignment of writing the final draft of the application. We were very fortunate in receiving this grant and receiving not only stipends for students, but also funds for the library and for faculty assistance.

At the beginning of my term as Director of Graduate Studies, I felt there was a need to review our admissions procedures. At that time, the chairman of each division made all decisions on the admission of students to master's and doctoral programs, subject to the approval of the Director of Graduate Studies. Students had complained that one person seemed to make a very important decision for them.

At a faculty conference, I suggested we try a committee within the division to review all graduate applications. Dr. Francis J. Crowley, who was serving as Chairman of the Division of Educational Psychology, Guidance, and Tests and Measurements, offered to form an admissions committee within his division. It worked so well that by the end of the year the other divisions followed suit.

As applications came to me for review, I sent some back to the committee with the request that they make sure candidates met the requirements set forth in the catalogue. Within two years the quality of the students accepted for admission improved considerably and the number of applications increased.

During the summer of 1962, I had a discussion with Dr. A. Paul Levack, who was the Dean of the Summer Session, about establishing a two-week course, called an institute, during the summer of 1963 in the field of educational administration and supervision. It was hoped that a two-week course given during the afternoons would attract people who had never taken courses at Fordham, but who felt a need to discuss problems they were facing, or expecting to face, in their school situations.

We had hoped for about 60 to 75 students, but by the opening day we had more than 120. We found that most of the students in that first institute applied to Fordham for matriculation in one of the University programs during the following year, and many who had come from out of town for the institute came back the following summer. After being appointed Director of Graduate Studies, I turned the conduct of the institute over to Dr. Anthony Baratta, who continued to conduct it for several years. The other divisions decided that the institute was a worthwhile course for the Summer Session and proceeded to establish institutes in the fields of reading, guidance, and special education.

FRANCES M. BLAKE

Frances M. Blake was a member of the Law School Class of 1945. She served as Executive Director of the Law School Alumni Association from 1964 to 1986.

Almost everybody finished school in two years in those days. Few people wanted to stay with the regular program. We dropped back and joined the incoming class the next semester. Then the following semester we joined the class half a year ahead of us. I don't know exactly how we did it, but we kept going with people who had started six months ahead of us or six months later. Because it was war time, we probably had more women than men, which was unusual.

I don't recall there being any particular alumni association while I was in law school. I think

Judge James B. M. McNally was the key person in starting it, or in revitalizing it. The first luncheon, in 1952 I believe, was the time they gave the Medal of Achievement to Judge Loughran. McNally was president from 1951 to 1953 and then Edward Shulkind came in and served as president until 1959, when Caesar Pitassy took over. Judge Hecht succeeded Pitassy in March of 1964, and that's when I began my work here. Prior to that, the association had been run out of the private office of the president, so I had to create an office and collect whatever records there were.

Judge Hecht was president for four years until 1968 and then Denis McInerney served from 1968 to 1972. Harry McCallion was president from 1972 to 1974—he would agree to only one term—and the famous John Feerick was president from 1974 to 1978. And then we had Jack Vaughn, Paul Curran, and now Jim Tolan.

The first thing I remember about John Feerick when he became president of the Alumni Association was that he came over to my office and wanted copies of everything. I didn't have copies of everything. Also, he wanted to know what kind of letters they wrote. I had written a lot of the letters myself, and the various presidents would okay them or write their own. Denis McInerney wrote a lot. But John was more for doing things himself in the beginning. Afterward he'd say, "Write this, write that."

John Feerick had me working from the word go. One year he was going off on vacation with his family, and he was going to be gone for two or three weeks. I thought I'd have a little relief here but then in the mail I'd get a long yellow legal-size sheet with writing on it in pencil telling me all these different things he had dreamed up for the alumni. He's up in a camp somewhere way up in Northern Canada and he had all these ideas of things he wanted me to be doing. So much for rest!

The Stein Award developed when Louis Stein went to John Feerick after Watergate with an idea to emphasize the positive side of the law or lawyers. Bill Frank spearheaded the formation of the award. The first one went to Judge Henry Friendly and was presented by Justice Thurgood Marshall. It was a very exciting affair, and we were all very pleased with the results. The University had had many such affairs, such as the President's Club Dinner and the like, but this was the first thing of that caliber we had run as an Association. When it came off so well it was very rewarding.

The Annual Luncheon used to be held the last Saturday before Ash Wednesday because people took fasting and not drinking and the like very seriously so they didn't want to have the luncheon during Lent. By the time I came aboard they had been fixed on the first Saturday of March. I think the best one I ever ran was when Judge Mulligan got the Achievement Award. He had just resigned from the Law School, but it was before he went on the bench. About a thousand people came.

The membership of the Association has grown quite a lot. I can remember when the total membership, dues-paying members, was only about a thousand. Now it's over 3,000.

GEORGE A. BROOKS

George A. Brooks, Fordham College Class of 1924 and Fordham Law Class of 1927, was an adjunct professor at the Law School from 1929 to 1935 and again from 1965 to 1985. He also served as President of the University Alumni Association and as Director of the Law School Alumni Association and was a member of the University Board of Trustees. He was awarded the Law Alumni Award of Achievement in 1968 and an honorary doctorate from Fordham in 1951. Mr. Brooks, who was an executive with General Motors from 1935 to 1965, died in 1988.

In my undergraduate days, clothing was much more formal than it is today. We wore a jacket, a collar, and a tie. Day-hops got their own food. In my senior year, we used to eat in a bakery and restaurant over on Third Avenue. We bought our books from the upperclassmen or from secondhand bookstores. There were three secondhand bookstores down on 59th Street, but if we were pressed, we would buy the books new.

The curriculum was essentially fixed. The basis for freshman and sophomore years was the humanities, and the classics and philosophy in junior and senior year. We also had courses in mathematics, history, chemistry, physics, and mechanics. The B.S. students took no Greek, but the A.B. students did.

Students basically made their own social functions. Dances were quite the usual event. The big social event in our four years was the junior prom held at the Biltmore Hotel. It was a very formal function with dance cards for your dance partners distributed.

I ultimately became editor-in-chief of *The Ram*, the student newspaper. The offices of *The Ram* were in what we used to call the Pill Box, which was later the Alumni House. We did all of our editorial work there. I think Father Ignatius Cox and then a Father McGrath were the faculty moderators. After we got all the copy together, we went down to the printers, which was someplace on West 39th Street in Manhattan.

As for religious activities, on First Fridays we went to Mass as a class. We had a St. Vincent

DePaul Society, and there was also a foreign missionary organization, the Harvester Club. During May, perhaps the outstanding event, the seniors would meet in the quadrangle in front of the statue of Our Lady and one senior each day would address the assembled group on some attributes of Our Lady. It was well done.

I believe we received our diplomas individually and the ceremony took place on Edwards Parade, but not facing east and west as is done now, but facing north and south, facing Freeman Hall.

At the Law School, which was located in the Woolworth Building at that time, we had an interesting study group of four. Bill Meagher, Joe Noble, Al Power, and I studied together each year, commencing with final exams during our first year. Bill Meagher became a founding partner of Skadden, Arps, Slate, Meagher & Flom, one of the most distinguished law firms in the City. Joe Noble became a partner in Bingham, Englar, Jones & Houston. Al Power became General Counsel of General Motors Corporation, and I became Secretary of General Motors and Director of the New York legal staff of GM.

We ate many of our meals at home, but Childs on Fulton Street had an interesting set-up if you didn't. The last table was, by custom, reserved for Fordham Law School night attendants and so if you came down late, you'd take a seat at the end table and get your meal then.

We had about ninety boys and just a few girls in the night school. One of the girls was Natalie McCarthy, who was a very bright, very jolly girl. John Finn, our Contracts professor, had given us a sample form of a contract and at the end of it were the letters "LS." So John Finn said, "Who knows what the letters L.S. mean?" The only one who knew was Natalie, who shot her hand up and said, "Locus signaturus." From that point on she was marked as an intellectual.

Professor Wormser had a hearing problem that was a bit ambiguous. When he called upon you, and after he had finished listening to what you had to say, or at least heard enough of your wisdom, he would turn the hearing aid off. If his questioning had been a little rough on the student and the student sat down muttering some imprecations under his breath, Professor Wormser, with his hearing aid turned off, would say, "What was that you said, Mister?"

HONORABLE JOHN M. CANNELLA

John M. Cannella graduated from Fordham College in 1930 and from Fordham Law School in 1933. He was a member of the football team during his undergraduate years, played for the New York Giants for two years after graduation, and is a member of Fordham's Football Hall of Fame. In July 1963, he was nominated by President John F. Kennedy to be a United States District Court judge, a position he held until 1977 when he took senior status. In 1965, he was given the Dean's Medal of Achievement by Fordham Law School.

Football—late 1920s

My memories of Fordham go back to February of 1926, and they are very precious indeed. My first knowledge that I would be going to Fordham occurred as a result of an incident involving my father and a man by the name of Ed Dugan. My father was a shoemaker, and Ed Dugan was one of his customers and an avid Fordham football fan. He was a student at Fordham Law School, and one of his classmates was Bill Ward, who was the line coach under Frank Gargan, the head coach of Fordham. Through the intervention of Bill Ward, I was offered a scholarship.

One of my first recollections after I entered Fordham was being examined by the school doctor, whose name, I believe, was Dr. Conboy. He lined up all the candidates alongside of the pool in the gymnasium, in military formation. When the doctor came to me, he remarked to his colleague, "This is a perfect specimen." My chest swelled with pride until I heard him end the sentence, which was "of flat feet."

The extent of my wardrobe when I entered Fordham was a pair of slacks, a few shirts, and a suede jacket which I received from my father. I was very proud of that jacket, so proud that apparently it bothered others. One day, as I was strolling near Fordham Road, I was hit in the back with a custard pie, from which the jacket never recovered.

The early part of my stay at Fordham was really divided into two sections. One while I played for Frank Gargan, and the other one I played under the "Iron Major," Frank Cavanaugh. When there was a change of coaches I lost my scholarship, and therefore had to pay my way. I continued to do that until one day when I was walking down to the Fordham path to the El station and I encountered Frank Cavanaugh walking toward me. He stopped me and asked, "Are you a student here?" "Yes," I said. "Well, why aren't you out for the football team?" I told him that I had lost my scholarship and was paying my own way and that I wasn't going to play unless I got my scholarship back.

He said, "If you make the team, I'll get your scholarship back." But I said, "No, if I come out for the team I want the scholarship now, and if I don't make the team, I'll pay for my way." So I went back again to try and make the team under Frank Cavanaugh, which I eventually did, and very happily he restored the scholarship and I was able to finish my studies at Fordham.

In the football season of 1929 we were playing Holy Cross in Worcester, Massachusetts. There was a fan in back of Coach Cavanaugh who kept shouting, "Put in Moko, Put in Moko." Moko was the son of the chief of police in Worcester, and he was on our team, but he was not a regular.

The shouting so angered Coach Cavanaugh that he got off the bench and ran up the stands after the fans and put a stop to the constant "Put in Moko, Put in Moko."

At the same time, someone shot off a cannon, which was interpreted as being the end of the game. There was still about ten minutes left to play and it was a very close game. It took the police considerable time to clear the field of spectators who had rushed out onto the field when they heard the cannon. Fortunately, we ended up with the victory, 7–6.

Many times in the course of the past years I've been asked whether I was on the "Blocks of Granite." Of course, the Blocks of Granite that got the most publicity were the ones who played under Jim Crowley, the so-called "Lombardi team." Actually, the Blocks of Granite designation, or expression, was first used for our team, the team of 1929. We had an undefeated team. The team was never scored upon through the line—the opposition only scored, when they did, through the forward pass. That's why we were referred to as the Blocks of Granite. The expression then took hold when the Crowley team came.

PETER A. CARLESIMO

Peter A. Carlesimo was a member of Fordham College's Class of 1940 and a teammate and close friend of Fordham football star Vince Lombardi, who later became the legendary coach of the Green Bay Packers in the National Football League. Carlesimo served as Fordham's Athletic Director from 1968 to 1978. He was also the Executive Director of the National Invitational Tournament from 1978 to 1988. He is widely recognized as one of the nation's premier after-dinner speakers. All ten of his children are graduates of Fordham, as are a nephew and two daughters-in-law.

The Class of 1940 was truly an outstanding group, and I am proud to be a member—men like Hank Smith, Ed White, Jim McGee, Ham DeCarlo, Wes Wallace, and Jack Barry. There were some great athletes in that class, especially in football. Dom Principe was a great fullback, and Billy Krywicki, an outstanding quarterback. Kazlo Steuc was a star halfback, and Wes Wallace was a nationally known runner. And Dan McGillicuddy was an excellent basketball player.

We had many outstanding class members who were stars in many other fields after graduation. I think of Donald Menagh, an attorney who was involved with the national labor unions, and Dr. Frank Loperfidd, who was our team doctor for many years. Professor Andy Myers of the Fordham faculty was a member of my class, and we had two judges from Connecticut, John Holiah and Jim McGrath. I remember Joe Daly, who was Chairman of Doyle, Paree, Barnbach Group, Inc. and a former Chairman of Fordham's Board of Trustees. Don McGanon, president of Westinghouse Communications Corporation, was a member of the Class of 1940 as was Dick Breen, who became famous as a writer in Hollywood. We had another attorney, Vic Cichahowicz, who became very prominent in international maritime law. I also remember two clergymen, now deceased, Joe Casey and Jim Cournean. Joe was a Jesuit and Jim was a Maryknoller.

The Jesuits ran a pretty tight ship. We had to be in our rooms by 7:00 P.M. From 7:30 to 10:00

was study period. Radios were not allowed until 10:00 P.M. Lights-out was at 11:00, and we had a nightly bed check.

The Jesuits were also great teachers. Men like Ignatius Cox and Joseph Murphy, as well as Father Anabell and Father Coniff, who later moved to Scranton University, where I joined him in 1942. Father Harold Mulqueen was a great figure on the campus. He was in charge of the band and was a prefect of the boarding facilities at St. John's Hall. Father Larry Walsh was outstanding as Dean of Studies. He was a great tennis player. And then there was Father Tyrean, who was a war hero. As Dean of Discipline, he was very strict, but very fair. Brother Quinn, also one of the major figures on the campus, was the "Major Domo" of the dining room. We tried to cultivate him as well as Brother Nolan, who was involved with the physical plant.

Over the years, speaking at more than 2,000 banquets, invariably I was introduced as one of the "Seven Blocks of Granite." But actually I was not since I was a freshman when they were seniors. It was a great line. The ends were Druze and Paquin; Ed Franco and Al Babartsky were the tackles; Vince Lombardi was the guard; the center was Alex Wojciechowicz, and Nat Pierce was the other guard. Wojie and Franco were two-time All-Americans. Lombardi became the

greatest coach in the history of pro football.

In addition to Vince Lombardi and many other football greats, I played two years with Jim Lansing. He starred in the Sugar Bowl game and also the Cotton Bowl game and then became my assistant for many yars. He was a great Fordham player and a great Fordham administrator who later coached club football.

After 26 years at the University of Scranton, I was not anxious to make a move. I can remember talking to my wife, Lucy, and I think we allowed six or seven of the children to vote as to whether I should stay in Scranton or come to New York and, believe it or not, New York got no votes whatsoever. But it was like coming home. Men like Lombardi, Tom O'Rourke, Dr. Meade, and Jack Mulcahy asked me to return. I did not apply for the job. I would not have left Scranton for any other position. When I came back, I replaced Johnny Bach. This was in August of 1968. John had moved on to Penn State as basketball coach.

I had dreams of Fordham someday coming back to big-time football. And I remember talking to Marie Lombardi and saying to her, "I wanted Vince to continue here at Green Bay for a couple of years and then I'd love to see him come back to Fordham as a coach and Fordham with big-time football, where I know the fans would respond with Vince as the head coach." She hugged me, she kissed me. She said, "He would love it."

When it was decided at Fordham that it was going to be too difficult to try to remodel the present structure for the gymnasium, that we were going to have to put up a new building, I called upon Vince to act as a chairman for a fund raising for the new gym and he responded, despite the fact that he was very, very busy. I remember he invited twelve men, very prominent men, who were going to act as the committee to raise the funds for the new gym at Fordham University. It could have been considered a Last Supper revival.

After Vince died of cancer in 1971, I then thought what we could do, instead of building a gym with him, now we would do it for him, and that's when the Vincent T. Lombardi Athletic Center became a reality. It would serve a vital function for students of the University and help Fordham attract more resident students at Rose Hill.

The builder for the gym was Anthony Dimallo, president of Terminal Construction, who contributed $1 million in construction material. I also remember Sal Naclerio, who was very much involved with the Board of Trustees. Fordham's President, Father James Finlay, made the great decision to go ahead. He was the key man or there wouldn't have been any gym. He was ably supported by Dr. Joseph Cammarosano, the Executive Vice President. I accompanied them to many other schools to learn whatever we could about arenas all over the country. We learned from the mistakes of others. We did not have unlimited funds, and what was to be a $4 million building turned out to cost $6 million. But it's been a great asset to Fordham.

KATHRYN I. SCANLON CARLIN

Kathryn I. Scanlon Carlin, a Professor Emeritus of Education, earned her B. S. from the Fordham School of Education in 1934, her Master's of Arts in 1936 and her Ph.D. from the School in 1956. From 1945 to 1974 she was the Director of Teacher Training, a title which was later changed to Director of Field Services and Teacher Certification.

Teachers College was the first School of Education at Fordham and was located on the 6th, 8th, and 28th floors of the Woolworth Building. We had the full four-year college come in 1930 to 1934 with the students right from high school. For those of us who were either working in industry or labs or who had come out of the normal schools, there were afternoon, evening, and Saturday classes. The Dean of the original Teachers College was Father Joseph Lennon, s.j.

When Teachers College became the School of Education and moved to 302 Broadway, Dr. Francis Crowley came as the first lay Dean. In fact, we were surrounded by Jesuits at the Woolworth Building. The only sizable group of lay people teaching in the Woolworth building were in the undergraduate Department of Education. They were mostly part-time people who were public school teachers who came in on Saturday to teach these courses.

Back in the 1930s, we paid $7 a credit for our undergraduate courses at Teachers College. When we came back one September they had raised it to $11 per credit hour. We were all going to quit. We were not about to fork up four more dollars, but we pretty soon found out that we wanted to stay there so we said, "Well, $4, we'll take it." They also charged a $5 registration fee that went for extracurricular activities. But we had no extracurricular activities. We would walk down to Battery Park for exercise. We had no socials, although we did go to an occasional football game.

The key philosopher in those days was Father Joseph Murphy, s.j., who scared the dickens out of us. Any philosophy and any basic concepts I have held onto since my college days I got from Father Murphy. He had a young assistant, Joe Sherlock, who would pinch hit every once in a while when Father Murphy couldn't make it down from the Bronx.

The famous Father Ignatius Cox would also come down from Rose Hill to teach economics. He was way beyond his time in economics, way beyond his time. He would come down on the Third Avenue Elevated train, all the way from Fordham Road, to teach us a two-credit course in economics, which was fabulous.

Leo Kearney, who received a 45-year medal from Fordham a few years ago, was my first education teacher. The brother of the Bishop of Rochester, James E. Kearney, he'd always say, "I am the brother of the Bishop of Rochester." He was a squat little Irishman who taught in New York City, I guess, all his adult life. He knew more about the insides of New York City and the methods of teaching than most anyone. He spurred me on to stay in education. He was an absolute gem. In fact, he made me feel like a professional in his courses from way back when.

Student life at 302 Broadway was quite different from the Woolworth Building. I can say that because I was young enough when I came to the School of Education as faculty to know the difference between the schools. I joined the staff in 1945 when we had men and women from World War II, taking advantage of the G. I. Bill. The School of Ed be-

came much more of a full-time co-ed student body than it had been before. At Teachers College, we saw one or two men floating through the halls, but it was mainly a women's college. With all the veterans, the whole complexion of the School changed. The activities had to be different and the conduct of the classes was different.

It was then that Father Robert Gannon was completing his tour as President of the University and Father Laurence McGinley became the President. I said, "Ah-ha, here's a young, vital man, tremendously interested in the School of Ed. We've got to let him know what the School of Ed is doing down here, or we better take the School up to the Bronx campus."

So once a year we used to take all the freshmen from the School of Ed up for a day on the Bronx campus and Father McGinley would meet us in his office. We would tour the campus. He came down to the School of Ed at least four to six times a year, to meet with the administration and the faculty and let everyone know he was interested in the School.

I was the person who recommended Dr. Harry Rivlin to become Dean of the School of Education. I suggested his name to Father Tim Healy, who was then Executive Vice President. After I approached Harry about the job, he said, "I'll go home and talk it over with {his wife} Jeanne." I said, "Okay, that's fair enough,

but get back to me tomorrow."
He said, "Tomorrow?" I said,
"Yes, I can't wait. If you don't
know tomorrow, you won't
know next week."

He called me at home that
night and said, "Kay, I'm interested." I said, "Good, I'll make
an appointment for you to go up
to see Tim Healy." He said,
"Who's Tim Healy? Is he a Jesuit?" I said, "Yes." He said, "Oh,
I don't know these fellows." I
said, "He won't bite you. It will
be fine." He went up, and Tim
Healy fell in love with Harry Rivlin. He said, "Harry, you've got
to come here." And he did.

The day that President Kennedy was shot I was teaching a
class in general methods on the
12th floor when a girl came to
my class to tell me Kennedy had
been shot. I stopped the class and
I said, "There's only one place to
go." We went down to the chapel
on the first floor and in those days
the students would follow you
right down. It was pretty well
crowded with students and I
started the Rosary. Halfway
through a girl came in and said
President Kennedy had died.
That to me was then most dramatic experience I ever had in my
life in that building. You could
have heard a pin drop in that entire building. The elevators didn't
seem to make any noise. Classes
were all called off and then we all
went home.

REV. W. NORRIS CLARKE, S.J.

Rev. W. Norris Clarke, S.J., was Professor of Philosophy at Fordham from 1955 to 1985. From 1961 to 1985, Father Clarke was the editor of International Philosophical Quarterly.

Even though this history goes back twenty-five years, it is easy to remember a project that has been one's own brainchild and into which one has poured so much of one's dreams, not to mention blood, sweat, and tears over so many years.

The idea was first conceived in 1958 by Father Joseph Donceel, S.J., a Belgian Jesuit who had become an American citizen and was teaching in the Fordham Philosophy Department, and proposed to myself, who had joined the Department in 1955, and to Father James Somerville, S.J.,

also teaching in the department. His idea was to begin a new philosophical journal that would be a collaborative venture between ourselves at Fordham and the Flemish Jesuits at the Jesuit House of Philosophical and Theological Studies at Leuven (the Flemish name for what we more commonly call over here the city and university of Louvain), in Belgium.

Father Donceel suggested that I should be the American editor-in-chief, and Father Frans De Raedemaeker, a distinguished philosopher, with wide acquaintances among European thinkers, the European editor.

The orientation of the journal would not be narrowly Scholastic or Thomistic, or even Catholic, but widely hospitable to a plurality of traditions. It would, however, favor the broad central tradition of theistic, personalist humanism, in dialogue between Europe and the Americas, and even more broadly between East and West.

I was not a little nervous about accepting the editorship, since I knew it would mean a great deal of work and involve some sacrifice of my own writing and scholarly career. But it did seem a truly apostolic enterprise and a typically Jesuit one, so I finally accepted it. Father De Raedemaeker in Belgium also accepted, with his Leuven colleagues.

Fordham's main concern was with our commitment to a long-range project and the financial support. The University was already subsidizing *Thought* and *Traditio* and did not feel it could take on another journal. When we agreed to take care of the financing ourselves by gathering an endowment fund, approval was given. It was agreed to publish all the articles in English—translating them where necessary—partly at the suggestion of a number of our Jesuit missionaries in Asia and Africa, who said English was now the common language for their people (especially in India, where the Belgian Jesuits had many contacts).

With the help of Father De Raedemaeker in Belgium we contacted and got promises of articles from some 50 or more philosophers of distinction around the world. Thus by the time we went into actual publication in 1961 we already had enough articles in hand for the whole first year. Especially during the first ten or fifteen years, but all through our career, Father Donceel has done most of the translation needed from German, French, and Dutch manuscripts—most now come in English.

The gathering of our endowment fund, to tide us over the years especially, was quite a task, one into which we all entered. But the real mastermind in this, who planned and carried out most of the work with great imagination and perseverance, was Father Somerville, who got in touch with a wide selection of Catholic foundations, distinguished Catholics from the *Who's Who* list, and others we thought would be sympathetic with our objectives. Over two years we raised something like $70,000, which seemed to us a safe enough cushion to go ahead and commit ourselves to actual publication.

Finally in February 1961 we came out with our first issue, printed in Belgium by the same printer who was already doing *Traditio*. Issues appeared regularly thereafter, first on a schedule of February, May, August, November, then after a few years into the more normal March, June, September, December sequence.

Our circulation rose steadily until after about six years or so it had reached a peak of about 2,000 annual subscribers, which placed us in the top dozen philosophical journals in the world in circulation at that time.

We suffered a severe loss at the start of our first year, 1961, when our European editor, Father Frans De Raedemaeker, died suddenly in Belgium. Father Maurice Huybens, s.j., of the same House of Studies in Leuven, agreed to take his place, and served us well until 1968, when his own health failed. He was replaced by Father Herman Morlion, s.j., Librarian of the same House, who worked with us until the entire Flemish House of Studies closed a few years later, due to the serious drop in religious vocations soon after Vatican II.

From the beginning *IPQ* was in fact an entirely Jesuit-owned and operated enterprise, with the consultation of the Fordham Philosophy Department but not under its control or management. Finally, in 1985, after completing twenty-five years as editor-in-chief, I retired from the direction of the journal and the Foundation. We elected Father Vincent G. Potter, s.j., of the Fordham Philosophy Department as the new editor and president of the Foundation.

JOHN J. COLLINS

Dr. John J. Collins is Professor Emeritus of History at The College at Lincoln Center. He retired in 1977. He began his Fordham career as an undergraduate in Fordham College, Class of 1930.

How I happened to enroll at Fordham University was almost coincidental. I attended a public high school in New York City, DeWitt Clinton, which *was* a very good school. I was president of the Newman Club, the club for Catholic students.

At that time, several college representatives interviewed graduating students to give them the highlights of their respective colleges. Father Charles Deane, s.j. then Dean of Fordham College, on such a recruitment mission spoke to the members of the Newman Club who were in their senior year, relating the advantages of attending Fordham College.

I was invited by Father Deane to visit the Fordham campus. Living, as I did, in the heart of Manhattan, I hardly knew where the Bronx was, and, of course, never visited the Fordham campus. When I did, I was very impressed. Father Deane personally escorted me around the campus including a visit to the new gymnasium. When I returned home, I persuaded my parents to allow me to attend Fordham. I never regretted their decision.

In my judgment, the Class of 1930 was unusual because of the number of gifted students in that class. It would be unfair to try to mention the names of all these outstanding students of which I was not one. My older brother, Bill, decided he too would like to attend Fordham. He made a special hit with everyone through his piano playing and singing.

Our class was known not just for its intellectual elite, but also for the fact that we could boast eight Reillys and eight Murphys. Nor shall we ever forget John Cannella's devastating tackle of the fleet N.Y.U. ball-carrying back, as he streaked down the field with the kick-off under his arm headed for a certain touchdown. Fordham defeated N.Y.U. 28–0. It was our first undefeated season. Cannella later became a federal judge, "tackling" and "passing on" the law.

Fordham was much smaller in the '20s than it is today. Father Deane, s.j., Dean of Students, could look out the window of his office in the Administration Building, and if he saw a student walking on the quadrangle, would come out and ask, "Why aren't you in class?" Today, Fordham's campus, in numbers, reminds one of Macy's basement. Students come and go endlessly.

The year 1926 (my freshman year) the Reserve Officers Training Corps (R.O.T.C). was established at Fordham. It was voluntary. About one-third of the class enrolled in R.O.T.C. I was among them. We were an anti-aircraft unit. When it came to marching, we certainly could not be compared to West Point Cadets or even Xavier High School cadets. When we drilled, as we passed Fordham Prep, many of the students would chant the "de reum de rump" in a mocking way, indicating how unmilitary we must have looked to them. Eleven of us enrolled in the advanced course of the R.O.T.C. for our junior and senior years. At graduation, we received commissions as Second Lieutenants.

Every class, of course, has had its unusual experiences—fascinating lectures, jokes, pranks, and the like. One experience that those of us of the Class of 1930 always recall, not just with nostalgia, but with reverence, was Father Joseph Murphy's psychology lectures—every morning for our entire senior year. The class

was held in the Administration Building. All 285 of us in one room were determined not to miss a word of Father Murphy's "pearls." For me it was the most intellectually stimulating class I've ever had—including many courses taken in graduate school.

One could hear a pin drop in that class, not because we feared Father Murphy, but because his lectures were studded with logical explanations of the most profound questions.

Rather than consider this just my personal observation, Dr. William McGill, who was in a later class at Fordham and who became President of Columbia University, wrote an article in *Fordham* magazine in which he said, even in his graduate work at Harvard and M.I.T. his outstanding professors there did not match Father Murphy.

This experience alone, in our senior year, was sufficient to have made Fordham a great university in the opinion of the Class of 1930.

There were no women on the campus at that time. We never thought much about it. There was no coeducation on the undergraduate level, that we knew of, in Catholic colleges. Some students had contacts at local colleges for women, such as Mount Saint Vincent and the College of New Rochelle. These were sources for partners at dances, Glee Club recitals, etc.

We, of course, always had a junior prom—until Cardinal

Hayes, then the Archbishop for the New York Archdiocese, forbade them, because of an incident involving students at another Catholic college, which he believed brought discredit on the Catholic college community (remember those were the days of Prohibition). "Proms" at Catholic colleges in the Archdiocese were thereafter banned.

Being ingenious, however, some of us set up "clubs" outside the Archdiocese. There was the Brooklyn–Long Island Club and the New Jersey Club where we continued to have our "proms." Father Deane came to these, understanding our judicious choice of facilities outside Cardinal Hayes's jurisdiction. He was a beloved Dean, with a wry sense of humor.

Any recollection of the days I spent at Fordham College—and this can be corroborated by my classmates—must include the mention of at least two lay professors who made an indelible impression on those who attended their classes: Professor Sam Telfair, a native of North Carolina, fascinating history professor, convert, and World War I decorated veteran, and Professor Julius Winslow who taught Pedagogy. Sam Telfair's lectures were more than stimulating. They were different in a way that evoked laughter, but prompted us to probe further.

Dr. Winslow taught Public Speaking to all of us in our freshman year. A white-haired, meticulously dressed gentleman, Dr. Winslow was just not prepared to handle New York City students with their witticisms and their pranks. When we get together, we recall with laughter and warmth the unusual lectures and other things that took place in Dr. Winslow's classes.

During our days at Fordham, many of us day-hops had part-time jobs—as waiters at Schraffts, working at Christmas time in the Post Office, Saturdays at Wanamakers or in the late afternoon throwing packages on trucks of the Railway Express Agency. Ten per cent of our classmates were boarders, mostly from Connecticut, Upstate New York, Pennsylvania, and Massachusetts.

Finally, at our Baccalaureate Mass, Father John White, Fordham Class of 1910, was the celebrant. He was well known for his marvelous sermons at St. Agnes Parish down on 43rd Street. I will never forget his advice to all of us—so simple and so true—"Whatever you do, no matter what happens in life, never lose your sense of humor."

When we graduated in 1930, the stock market crash of 1929 had already ushered in the Great Depression. And although it did not end until World War II, we managed. Above all, Fordham gave us an orientation that enabled us to navigate through the shoals of economic adversity and WW II, so as to enjoy the fruits of better times during the many years since our graduation.

"Hail, Men of Fordham," and
now, also, "Hail Women of Fordham."

RALPH R. DeMAYO

Ralph R. DeMayo, a former New York City police officer, has been the Director of Alumni Relations at Fordham since 1976. He earned his master's degree in social group work from Fordham in 1951 and served as an adjunct assistant professor in the School of Social Service from 1957 to 1963. From 1964 to 1969 he was the Senior Associate Director of Development at Fordham.

In 1949 I was accepted in the School of Social Service and had my interview with Dr. Anna King. She was a beautiful person, a real, warm, bright, congenial leader. It was interesting since she then assigned us the task of going to see the movie *Monsieur Vincent*, in French, the life of St. Vincent de Paul, and then we had to write an essay on what it meant to us. I still have that one at home. I found it recently while going through my papers, but it is indicative of the type of approach that Anna King had in working with new students.

In those days the School was located at 39th Street and Lexington Avenue. I can remember coming to school one morning and being greeted by Father Joseph T. O'Brien, S.J., who was the Regent. He was beside himself. The custodian was not in, and the fire was going out. There was concern that the pipes would burst. It was wintertime, and he had Al Olson, another police officer who was going to school at the time, and me down in the basement trying to stoke the furnace and get the fire going.

I am also reminded of the days when I was president of the Alumni Association, and we used 39th Street for our meetings. Your task as president was to get there before five o'clock so you would have control of the door, let everyone in, and get your room set up. At the end of the evening, you let everyone out and locked that big heavy iron door. Then you went downstairs and went out the lower exit in order to leave the building. It was a very interesting spot. It was warm and supportive. It was also a lot of stair-climbing.

There were some outstanding individuals at 39th Street. At Commencement now we have the Dr. Curren Award and everyone asks, "Who is Dr. Curren?" Dr.

Curren was our everything man. He was the registrar, financial aid officer, and admissions officer all rolled into one. And he was a little deaf. Now, if you came into his room and said you needed some leeway in paying your tuition or something, he would take care of it. But always as a deaf person would have it, it was at the top of his lungs, and most people anywhere in earshot could hear what was going on. He was a beautiful man, and it's a shame that we don't give a better picture of him when we present the award.

When I went to work for the Development Office, it was located on the 42nd floor of the Chrysler Building. It occupied one-half of that floor. We ran our program there until we moved to the Administration Building in 1966. We closed the main office in the Chrysler Building, and moved the whole operation up to campus. We stayed there until 1968, when we moved down here to the third floor at Lincoln Center. The Alumni Office did not move to Lincoln Center until 1975.

Father Finlay felt the Alumni Office was better located here at Lincoln Center than in its little Pill Box on campus. One of the reasons Father John Connolly of sainted memory then submitted his resignation, and the reason that Father Finlay called me to say "Ralph, I'd like you to be my Director of Alumni Relations," was that Father Connolly did not like having to come down to the city every day. He preferred his spot up on campus.

The Office of Alumni Relations has grown rather dramatically. When I first came here in 1976, I had an assistant, Jack Jacklin, a fine man, a secretary, a secretary for Jack, and a bookkeeper. There were five of us. My present staff for alumni is five assistants, Father Jaskievicz, an Associate Director; Ed Buckley, a Deputy Director; Marina Venizelos, an Associate Director; Celeste Manuli and Kathleen Kelley, who are Assistant Directors; and five secretaries.

In addition to this, I have inherited the gift-posting operation, the gift-acknowledgment operation, and then I have a new unit that I've developed for database maintenance. So I now have a staff of 22. It's grown rather large with diverse responsibilities. We run a pretty comprehensive program in the Alumni Office. We run an event on the average of one every other day.

REV. FREDERICK C. DILLEMUTH, S.J.

Rev. Frederick C. Dillemuth, S.J., a graduate of the Class of 1944 from Fordham College, has been a member of the Department of Chemistry at Fordham since 1960 and Professor of Chemistry since 1984. He has served two terms as Chairman of the Department, from 1968 to 1971 and from 1984 to 1990.

What I have to say about the Medical College is what I heard from my father, who graduated from there in 1913. I cannot vouch for the accuracy of these statements, just for the fact that this is what I recall my father telling me.

The school was last housed in what is now Finlay Hall. It was built as the new Medical School. The original Medical School was in Thebaud Hall, which afterward became the School of Pharmacy. The Medical School, as all

medical schools, was a very costly operation, even in the early 1900s. Therefore, there might have been some desire on the part of the Administration to let the Medical School go since it was draining the University's resources.

Another central issue at that time was that Fordham did not own its own medical school hospital. That would have been the desired situation. However, it would have been very expensive to acquire a hospital that would be under the University's control.

Finally, Fordham had about all it could bear with regard to the free hemorrhaging of funds necessary to keep the Medical School going. It also did not want to run a medical school with a B rating. (The B rating was proposed by the Flexner Report for any university that did not own its own hospital.) Consequently, it was decided to close the School. There were efforts on the part of various alumni and other interested groups to try to gather enough money to keep things going and to establish an endowment but these were not too successful on the whole.

When I was a freshman in college here in 1940, Father Gannon remarked that the University had been offered $1 million which at that time would have been sufficient to keep the school open and $10 million more as an endowment. The donors, however, wanted to have some control over admissions and teaching. At that time, it was unheard of that an operation under the auspices of the Jesuits would not be under their complete control. The money was, therefore, refused. My father was a member of one of the groups that tried to collect money and pledges to reopen the school. His group was rather successful. They were finally told by the Administration to stop their efforts since Fordham had no plans to reopen the school.

During the early 1900s there was an effort on the part of some medical schools to limit the representation from various ethnic groups. This did not occur at Fordham. Fordham was very open in its admissions policies and did not put quotas on ethnic and religious groups. And I think that is why a lot of people wanted the Fordham Medical School to be kept alive, since it did not discriminate and did open its doors to people who were not Catholics or necessarily white Anglo-Saxons.

It was a pity the place was closed. On the other hand, to open it again now would just be out of the question. There were, I think at the time when Father Vincent O'Keefe was Rector–President, in the early 1960s, feelers put out by the Archdiocese whether or not Fordham would be willing to open the Medical School again. This might have been when the diocese was thinking of buying New York Medical College, now located at Valhalla, New York. I suspect it wanted the Medical College to be affiliated with Fordham. When asked about it by Father O'Keefe, I felt that unless a substantial amount of money were put up front, it would not be a wise idea. Still, if Fordham could have maintained the Medical School, it would have been a feather in its cap.

My father never had any regrets that he came here. Though he started off at New York University he later transferred to Fordham. In his senior year, he won the prize for the best essay on gastroenterology, $25 in gold. He had planned to go to Austria to start post-graduate studies on the first of September 1914, but World War I broke out. When the hostilities continued with no end in sight, he settled in the Bronx.

On Saturdays and Sundays when my brothers and I were not in school, he would take us along to stay in the car and watch it while he made house calls. Every time we drove past Fordham he told me that that was the place I was going to go to college. I took the scholarship exam because I was told I was going to take it. It was a two-day exam, early in June of 1940. I had never taken an exam as hard as that in all my life. I was convinced that I had gone right through the bottom.

Well, a week or two later, on a Saturday morning, while I was still in bed, I heard a yell downstairs. I thought Mom was in trouble so I jumped out of bed and ran down. The mail had come. Now, in those days kids seemed to have no privacy or rights. Mom had opened the letter from Fordham informing me that I had won the Frank Leary Manning Scholarship, an $800 award. This, together with a New York State scholarship for $400, paid for four years tuition, which was $300 per year at that time.

When my father came downstairs my mother told him, "Freddy just won a scholarship to Fordham." Pop told me, "Get dressed; you are going to accept it." And that is how I started at Fordham.

REV. G. RICHARD DIMLER, S.J.

Rev. G. Richard Dimler, S.J., has been teaching German at Fordham since 1972. He is a 1956 graduate of Fordham College and earned his Master's in education from Fordham in 1960. Since 1978 he has been the editor of Thought.

The Origin and History of *Thought*

Much of the original history of *Thought* can be found documented in the volume put out by Father Joseph E. O'Neill called *Fifty Years of Thought* (Fordham University Press, 1978).

The project of publishing a Catholic quarterly of the sciences and letters was discussed frequently during the first half of the 1920s. This was at a time when a new period of Catholic intellectual activity was begin-ning. The moment seemed opportune for a new advance beyond the journalistic and the popular, and even some of the cultured periodicals then in existence. Catholic progress called for the establishment not only of a literary quarterly for cultivated readers, but also for an organ through which specialists could speak to scholars and research students. With these considerations in mind, Wilfred Parsons, s.j., then Editor-in-Chief of *America*, and Francis P. LeBuff, s.j., then Dean of the School of Social Service at Fordham, decided that a quarterly should be inaugurated. In June of 1926, *Thought: A Quarterly of the Sciences and Letters* published its first issue.

Reaction to the name "Thought" throughout the years has, by and large, been favorable. It was suggested by Leo J. Gilleran, a second-year theologian at Woodstock College in Maryland, the former Jesuit House of Studies for philosophy and theology. Its descriptive title has since been changed to "A Review of Culture and Idea." To the occasional objection of the disapproving few, that the name "Thought" is unwarranted and even boastful, there has always been the reasonable response, "Nonsense! It's short. It's easy to remember."

The quarterly's first issue of 188 pages of large, clear type carried nine articles, two pages of illustrations, one poem, and four book reviews. There was no fiction, and there never has been any fiction in *Thought*. The lead article was written by Peter Gilday, a well-known Catholic historian, and entitled "The Catholic Church in the United States: A Sequicentennial Essay" It was a rousing salute to the country and to the role of the Catholic Church in its development.

Wilfred Parsons served as editor from 1926 to 1936 and was succeeded until 1939 by Francis Talbot, who served as editor of *America* as well. Most of the contributors, as one would expect, were drawn from the Catholic community, and most were Americans, with some English and French. Some were well known, or were soon to become so: Jacques Maritain, Fulton Sheen, Donald Atwater, Theodore Maynard, Sister M. Medlayba, Helen Peter Eden, and, among the Jesuits, Herbert Thurston, André Bremon, Paul Blakely, and Pedro Arrupe, the future General of the Society of Jesus.

By the year 1939, *Thought*, now a teenager, was ready for a new and expansive life. Thus, it found, owing to the foresight and energy of Robert I. Gannon, President of Fordham University, its transferral from *America* and the America Press to Fordham and the Fordham University Press. It was a good move because it guaranteed the continued life of the rapidly growing journal.

At first intended primarily as an outlet for the writings of the various members of the Fordham faculties, it quickly opened its pages to other scholars, both Catholic and non-Catholic, outside Fordham, at home and abroad. With the issue of March 1940, *Thought* made its first appearance as the quarterly of Fordham University, and the new editor was Gerald G. Walsh, S.J., a graduate in Classics from the University of London and a First Class Honorsman in History at Oxford University. A man of boundless energy, he quickly proved himself to be an outstanding editor during these years of expansion. The areas of greatest interest were now political philosophy, politics, and policy, with a stress on such issues of the day as war, military service, problems of peace, Europe and European unity, Communism, Fascism, Nazism, and nationalism.

In 1950 Father Walsh was succeeded as editor by a fellow Jesuit, William F. Lynch. Under his vigorous editorship, *Thought* widened the range of its contributors to include well-known scholars, especially in the literary field, including W. H. Auden, Marshall McLuhan, and Walker Percy, and, in other fields, such well-known people as Gustav Weigel, Thomas Merton, and Frank Sheed.

In 1956, Joseph E. O'Neill, S.J., a member of the English Department at Fordham University, assumed the editorship of *Thought*. Father O'Neill continued as editor for twenty years and is credited with the establishment of the Founders and Associates of *Thought*. The generous financial aid and moral support of these faithful friends have been of invaluable assistance.

The major source of financial backing for *Thought* from 1940 on has been, of course, the various presidents of Fordham University itself. Their support has provided a security blanket over the years, despite the news in April 1968, when the Editor learned that, in the interest of economy, *Thought* was to be discontinued. However, Father O'Neill launched a decisive counter-attack. Consultants from outside the University were asked to evaluate *Thought*, and with their judgment proving highly favorable, the decision was made that it would be allowed to continue. The quarterly resumed its calm existence when its first non-Jesuit editor, Joseph E. Grennen of the Fordham English Department, took over. Professor Grennen carried on admirably until my own appointment in 1978, and I have been editor since that time.

Among the articles I would consider outstanding are the following: John Tracy Ellis' "American Catholicism, 1953–1959: A Notable Change," which appeared in the June 1979 issue; Avery Dulles' seminal article "Imaging the Church for the 1980s," in June 1981; Joseph Cardinal Bernardin's article for the special issue on nuclear morality called "A Consistent Ethic of Life: An American Catholic Dialogue"; and Andrew Greeley's article on the making of a storyteller.

REV. JOSEPH DONCEEL, S.J.

Rev. Joseph Donceel, S.J., a native of Belgium, was a member of the Philosophy Department at Fordham from 1950 until 1972. Prior to that he served for six years as Assistant Professor in the Psychology Department. Since 1975 he has been Professor Emeritus.

The intellectual atmosphere at Fordham when I arrived was, in the Departments of Theology and Philosophy, the atmosphere of a seminary. The College professors in these departments were all Jesuits. They taught the Fordham students what they had been taught at the Jesuit theologate at Woodstock, Maryland. So it was rather simple, not on a scholarly level, but very solid.

There were, in the Philosophy Department, outstanding people on the graduate level. There was Dr. Pegis, who had a great reputation as a philosopher and who eventually went to Toronto to the {Pontifical} Institute of Mediaeval Philosophy. Later there was Dr. Dietrich von Hildebrand, who was world-famous in philosophy. There was Dr. Robert O. Pollock, who, although he had written very little, had a great influence because he was a very nice man and had a tremendous erudition. There was also Dr. Elizabeth Salmon, who would eventually be elected president of the American Catholic Philosophical Association.

I may have been instrumental in a change in the way philosophy was taught at the University. The philosophy being taught was Thomism, as understood by Jacques Maritain and Etienne Gilson. I started teaching Thomism as understood by Scheuer, Maréchal, and Karl Rahner, taking with them the "transcendental turn," which, although first clearly introduced by Kant, had occasionally been used already by Aristotle and St. Thomas. So what came to be called "Transcendental Thomism" may well, in this country, have had its humble beginnings in my classes and my textbooks.

The intellectual level of the Fordham College Philosophy Department began to rise first under the impulsion of a new dean, Father Thurston Davis. It continued to rise steadily as the powerful efforts made by the Jesuits began to pay off. They had been sending some of their brightest young men to the very best universities in the States and Europe, and as these men arrived, the changes began to appear.

First (and not only chronologically!) came Father Norris Clarke. He had studied philosophy in a French Scholasticate and at the University of Louvain. At Fordham he developed into one of the leading Catholic philosophers of this country. Fathers Quentin Lauer and Robert O'Connell came from France's Sorbonne. They began to introduce new methods which, at first, were not welcomed by their colleagues. Their Thomism had weakened and died in France.

But after a while some of us began to realize that it was rather doubtful whether the Church had a right to impose upon schools that were not seminaries, that were not forming its future priests, the doctrine of St. Thomas as the only safe one. What these newcomers were trying to do was really in the line of a solid new development that had already started in the Graduate School.

Although the philosophy course looked very much like a seminary course, the students really liked it. At the end of the year, *The Ram*, the student paper, would take some kind of an informal poll asking the students which was their favorite course, and almost every year it was overwhelmingly philosophy. They had a great number of hours of philosophy. If I'm not mistaken, five hours a week in junior year and ten hours a week in senior year, and they attended these courses in senior year formally dressed in their gowns. If they did not have their gown, they were politely asked to leave the classroom, because an intellectual banquet supposed also that you were dressed for a banquet.

The reason, I think, why they liked that course so much is that it gave them a solid conception of life based not only on religion or faith, but on reason. Many of these students had gone to Catholic kindergarten, grammar school, and high school. So they had been studying theology, if you may call it that, since they were kiddies. It is difficult then to continue to make that interesting. Whereas philosophy for them was a brand new world.

I believe that St. Ignatius would have preferred the old seminary style to the present university style. We used to read a rule taken from his *Constitutions* according to which all of us should say the same thing and think the same thing and different doctrines ought not to be permitted, either orally in sermons, or public lectures, or in books. However, although this injunction seems to exclude scholarship, St. Ignatius himself, as Karl Rahner has frequently pointed out, has proposed and defended an important new doctrine: that at times and especially in the course of the

Spiritual Exercises, God Himself speaks directly to the soul, by means of spiritual consolation, or the lack of it. Ignatius might be surprised if he came to Rose Hill. Would not St. Peter be surprised if he came to the Vatican?

MARGARET E. DONNELLY and
VIRGINIA STAUDT SEXTON

Dr. Margaret E. Donnelly is a 1937 graduate of Fordham College, Manhattan Division, who earned her M.A. (1940) and Ph.D. in Psychology (1973) from Fordham's Graduate School of Arts and Sciences at Rose Hill. She went on to be a Professor of Psychology at Pace University in Manhattan.

Dr. Virginia Staudt Sexton earned her master's and doctoral degrees at Fordham University. She was a lecturer in the Adult Education program from 1952 to 1954. She is a Professor Emeritus of the City University of New York and Distinguished Professor of Psychology at St. John's University, Jamaica, N.Y.

[Their reminiscences of their Fordham experience include remembrances of two outstanding teachers in the early years of the Department of Psychology, Rev. Walter G. Summers, S.J. (1889–1938), the founder and director of the Psychology Department in the Graduate School from 1934 to his death in 1938, and Dr. Joseph F. Kubis (1911–1982).]

DR. DONNELLY: I first met Father Summers about 1935 while an undergraduate student at Fordham College, Manhattan Division. Philosophy was my major, and after having taken all the philosophy courses in the catalogue, I thought I needed some guidance for future study. I found Father Summers attentive and receptive to my request, and he permitted me to take graduate courses in psychology, which I then proceeded to do. My first impression of Father Summers was that of a brilliant, dedicated, warmly human person.

The first Psychology Department headquarters in 1933 were located in a large two-room suite on the seventh floor of the Woolworth Building in Manhattan. These served as office, laboratory, and a store room for equipment. The atmosphere was highly informal and discussions often intense. One of the early students was Joseph Kubis, who was studying for his Ph.D. and doing some teaching there. Others were Fabian Rouke, Tim Costello, Mr. Zegers (later Father Zegers), Elizabeth Kelly, Beatrice LeCraft, and myself.

The Department moved to the beautiful, newly opened Keating Hall in the summer of 1937. We had a large fully-equipped experimental laboratory and a two-semester course in Experimental Psychology was required of all students. Dr. Kubis (he had attained his Ph.D. in June 1937), together with Father Summers, had prepared a laboratory manual, and we all worked our way through the experiments. Next to the laboratory was the library, consisting mostly of Father Summers' books and journals, which he freely lent to us.

We always regarded Joseph Kubis as the heir-apparent of Father Summers, and I think those of us who have studied with Dr. Kubis over the years felt that to be so, too.

DR. SEXTON: I had heard a great deal about Father Summers and about the Psychology Department and so, in January 1938, I went up to register. I had studied the catalogue very carefully and the course I wanted to begin with was Psychology of Mysticism. Father Edward Bunn, substituting for Father Summers, who had just suffered a heart attack, looked at me and he said, "Oh now, Miss Staudt, you can't take that course. You'll have to take statistics, systematic psychology, and since you are a graduate of Hunter College, you're going to have to take fundamentals of philosophy, so you won't be taking Psychology of Mysticism for a long time."

That was a bit of a letdown, but that was my introduction to Father Bunn, who later became President of Georgetown University. The first course that I took that spring was Systematic Psychology, and again Father Bunn was the teacher for the course for six weeks, until Father Summers returned from his convalescence. He completed the course for us.

That was my first course in the Department, and it was a wonderful experience but unfortunately, the following September, in 1938, Father Summers died.

REV. JOHN W. DONOHUE, S.J.

Rev. John W. Donohue, S.J., a 1939 graduate of Fordham College, joined the faculty of the School of Education in 1955 and taught in the Division of History and Philosophy of Education until 1969. He was Dean of Thomas More College frorm 1963 to 1966 and served three terms on the University's Board of Trustees (1969–1977, 1978–1984, and 1986–1989).

On September 27, 1963, Father Vincent O'Keefe, the President of Fordham, called me into his office for an interview. Father O'Keefe had become President of Fordham and the Rector of the Fordham Jesuit Community in June of that year, after having served for three years as Academic Vice President. Father O'Keefe told me that he wanted me to be the Dean of a new col-

lege that would enroll women on the Bronx campus and have a program almost exactly parallel to that of Fordham College. But it would be, at least on paper, a distinct college from Fordham College.

For many years, Fordham had provided undergraduate eduation for women, but only downtown at the School of Education. In fact, the young men and women in the School took, along with the professional courses in education, a program of liberal arts more demanding than is required now in most liberal arts colleges in this country. But they did not receive the A.B. degree, only a B.S. degree.

As I recall the history of the early '60s, there was a committee on the Fordham campus—the late Father Charles Loughran may have been its chairman—that proposed creating a new undergraduate college on the Bronx campus. It would have lower admissions standards than Fordham College, would admit both men and women, and would admit a large class—perhaps as many as a thousand. So some cynic said what they were planning was a college for dollars, dolls, and dokes.

But Father O'Keefe decided on a much smaller college, just for women and with the same admissions requirements as Fordham College, or ones even more demanding.

I always considered myself singularly ill-qualified for that position and I used to try to explain why I was chosen. I said, this college was going to enroll, as it actually did, gifted, highly qualified young women, but young women from middle-class families of German-American, Irish-American, Italian-American, and Polish-American backgrounds who would be the first of their families to go to college. In order to reassure their parents that this was a safe and trustworthy enterprise, they chose as the first dean somebody who looked like Cardinal Spellman, and thereby could reassure the parents and project a kind of sound image.

The idea was that I would spend the academic year 1963–1964 preparing for the coming of the first class to Thomas More College, in the fall of 1964. One of the first things to do was check on the physical facilities for this new college. I was given an office on the second floor of the Administration Building. I was also given a secretary, Mrs. Dorothy O'Connell, who had a desk just outside the door of my office.

The second critical need was to secure a qualified woman as the Assistant Dean. I would think it was just a stroke of luck, or perhaps I should say a blessing of divine providence, that we did in fact, though we scarcely knew how we were going about it, secure an excellent Assistant Dean.

When Father O'Keefe and I were beginning our search, he gave me a small leaflet put out by the American Association of University Women, and it advertised the services of what it called its roster. By that I think it meant nothing more than a filing cabinet in its office with résumés of its members. They sent us a number of résumés, and I recall interviewing three women. One of them was Patricia R. Plante.

She was born in 1932 and had taken a Ph.D. from Boston University in 1962. In that academic year of 1963–1964 she was teaching English at the University of Bridgeport. I interviewed her in February of 1964. She was extremely gifted for university work. She was a crackerjack teacher, admired by both men and women students. She also had the kind of personality that made her the sort of teacher in whom both men and women students found it easy to confide.

She would later become the second Dean of Thomas More College. What happened was that Father Leo McLaughlin, who in September 1965 succeeded Father Vincent O'Keefe as President, called me into his office in June of 1966 and fired me from that job. I think he was quite right in doing so. I don't think I was a particularly successful Dean or particularly well qualified to be a Dean of a women's college. I think he made an intelligent and very practical decision in thinking it would be better to have someone else. I was succeeded by Dr. Plante, who served until June of

1968. She brought that first class to its graduation.

I always considered finding Dr. Plante as one of my best contributions to Thomas More College. Another was to launch the Fine Arts Department with Dr. Irma Jaffe as its first chairperson and Dr. James Kurtz, who was in charge of the music courses.

REV. AVERY DULLES, S.J.

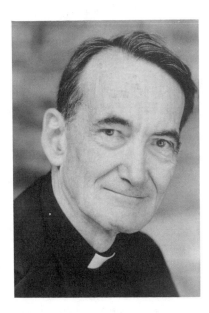

Rev. Avery Dulles, S.J., was appointed in 1987 as the first Laurence J. McGinley Professor of Religion and Society, a position he has occupied since 1988. A convert to Catholicism, Father Dulles is one of the pre-eminent theologians in the Church. Father Dulles retired in 1988 after 14 years on the faculty of The Catholic University of America in Washington, D.C.

I've been conscious of Fordham university ever since I came into the Church in the fall of 1940. I was instructed in the faith by Father Edwin Quain, who shortly after that became a professor at Fordham. I used to visit him in the early 1940s, and I remember attending the Summer School of Catholic Action at Rose Hill in the summer of 1941. Then in my regency years as a Jesuit Scholas-

tic, I was an instructor in philosophy here from 1951 to 1953. I came back frequently after 1960 for summer school programs, and I taught a course at Fordham in the spring of 1970. From 1969 to 1972, when Father Michael Walsh was President, I served on the Board of Trustees.

I received my appointment to the McGinley Chair from Father Joseph O'Hare, Fordham's President, in a letter dated April 9, 1987. Father O'Hare described the position in these words: "It would be a University professorship, not identified with any one department or even any one school; instead the McGinley professor would have the greatest possible freedom in working with people here at Fordham. Similarly, we thought that designating the Chair as a Chair in Religion and Society would allow us the freedom to interest scholars from a variety of disciplines in coming to Fordham in this capacity."

Father O'Hare went on to say, "Since Father McGinley's own discipline was theology and since he was, before coming to Fordham, a member of the Woodstock Theological Faculty, I believe that it would be particularly appropriate if the first occupant of the Chair were to be a theologian and a Jesuit. This is obviously not a necessary criterion and I assume that in future years scholars from other disciplines and non-Jesuits would surely be invited to fill the McGinley Chair."

One of the duties of the Mc-Ginley Professorship is to deliver a semi-annual lecture modeled after the annual Gannon Lecture Series. For my first such lecture, in December of 1988, I chose the topic "University Theology as a Service to the Church." My theme was that the doctrine of the Church needs to be stated and explained in a way that is abreast of current knowledge and in relationship to other disciplines and specializations. The University, therefore, has the unique capacity to update the formulation of theology and the theological explanation of doctrine in dialogue with other fields of study such as history, philosophy, psychology, and sociology. Before the Second Vatican Council, the theology that was taught on campuses was largely a watered-down version of seminary theology.

For my next lecture, in the spring of 1989, at the suggestion of Rev. William V. Dych, s.j., Chairman of the Theology Department, I chose an ecumenical theme and format. The topic chosen was "Authority and Freedom in the Church." We had a Lutheran bishop, William Lazareth, Bishop of New York of the Evangelical Lutheran Church in America, and the other participant was Father John Meyendorff, who teaches at St. Vladimir's Orthodox Seminary and also at Fordham. We had a good three-way ecumenical discussion on the topic of authority in the Church.

As the McGinley Professor, I have also taught a seminar each year. In the fall semester, 1988, I led a seminar which I entitled "Faith and Subjectivity." It consisted largely of critical reading of four authors on the subject of faith: Thomas Aquinas, John Henry Newman, Maurice Blondel, and Pierre Rousselot. In the spring of 1990, I conducted a seminar entitled "Questions in Ecclesiology," which explored the relationship between the Pope and the bishops. I examined the principle of collegiality and how it works out in certain new institutions such as the synod of bishops and the episcopal conferences.

I have done extensive research and writing about John Henry Newman, the nineteenth-century theologian, and so my McGinley Lecture in the fall of 1990 was entitled "Newman, Conversion, and Ecumenism." The lecture commemorated the centenary of Cardinal Newman's death on August 11, 1890. An Anglican who converted to Catholicism as an adult, Newman combined loyal adherence to the Catholic Church with a concern for Christian unity.

My appreciation for Newman has grown over the years, but in my early years as a convert to Catholicism, although I knew of him, I didn't identify with him very much. He came from a very different experience in high Anglicanism and the kinds of problems he worked on were not mine. The things that were difficulties for him were not difficulties for me. Things that were obvious to him were not obvious to me, and therefore the kind of conversion experience that he described in his autobiography was quite different from mine.

A number of Catholic authors influenced me as I made my way into the Catholic Church. Etienne Gilson and Jacques Maritain were two of the most influential, and I read everything by them that I could get my hands on. There were also a great number of prominent converts and apologists writing in that period, especially in England, whom I also read.

The ecumenical movement today is going forward, but not at a dramatic pace. Right after Vatican II, there was a lot of misunderstanding to be cleared up and the churches were discovering each other. It was a very exciting time in ecumenism. I think we now know each other fairly well, but there are still some stereotypes that need to be questioned and we don't really understand fully the reasons why we differ on the points where we do differ.

So there's a need for ongoing theological discussion, not only between the Catholic and Lutheran Churches, but among all the churches. With a will to unity we can in time, I think, overcome many of the divisions and achieve a great deal of common commitment and collaboration among the churches, even if we don't succeed in achieving full visible unity.

DONALD M. DUNN

Donald M. Dunn graduated first in the Fordham Law School Class of 1928. He was a Director of the Law School Alumni Association from 1952 to 1989 and was then elected its first Director Emeritus. He received the Law School Alumni Award of Achievement in 1974.

My identical twin brother, Ronald, was responsible for my choosing the law. He and I were pre-med students at Holy Cross. I was a good student and he was too, except that when he got into pre-med, he decided after one year that wasn't for him. I was admitted to Harvard Medical School and Jefferson Medical School, but I too was having some reservations about medicine as a career. We had been through all of our preliminary schools together and were never separated. He decided that he wanted to go to law school. This was late in the year of 1925. My contribution to medicine was that the man who took my place in Harvard became one of the top neurosurgeons of the country.

Entry into Fordham Law School was not as difficult in those days as it is today. We both got into Fordham Law School, evening division, and fortunately that division was the first one they had up at Rose Hill. It was reportedly made up of all college graduates for the first time because up until then it had been possible to get into Fordham Law School with two years of college and some preliminary training or whatever, but I think that almost everybody who was in our class was a college graduate. We thought we were a very special group, and we were.

I should mention Professor Joseph F. Crater. He taught us Corporate Law and was quite a character. We had Professor Keefe. He was a good friend of mine. I remember when he ran for Municipal Court Judge in Queens County. He said that he lost mostly because the Irish over there couldn't understand why he wasn't O'Keefe instead of Keefe. We had Professor Butler in Real Estate. Good ones. And, of course, Judge Loughran taught New York Practice—a wonderful teacher.

We had a fellow in our class who chewed tobacco. Crater, in

ordinary course, would call for a recitation alphabetically but he picked this fellow out of order. I'll never forget it. "McGlinchey, tell us more about this case we're discussing, what your thoughts on it are." McGlinchey was chewing tobacco—he didn't expect to be called on—but he calmly went over to an open window and spat out the window (ground floor) and then went back and answered the question. Crater loved that performance.

We continued there for three years, and when we finally came to the end of our three-year course, I graduated first in my section, first in my class, and first in the whole school—with Ronald close behind.

Then my twin and I were in a debate about what we would do about practicing law and where. We came from Oneida, New York, which is between Syracuse and Utica and the geographical center of the state. A small city, but it was, of course, our city. In the course of making that big decision I received a call from Professor Carr at Fordham Law. He told me that Alexander & Green, one of the most prestigious firms in the City, was looking for someone with good marks and so on.

I was interviewed by one of the partners at lunch. He took me back to the offices of Alexander & Green, then at 120 Broadway. That firm was organized in 1843, and I was the first Fordham man that had even been considered.

This partner took me to the managing partner. He asked, "Where did you go to college?" I said I went to Holy Cross. "How did you do there?" I said I was magna cum laude. He said "How did you do at Fordham?" I said I was number one in my class. He said "When can you start?" Marks are important!

I was immediately put into litigation and eventually I became the head of litigation in Alexander & Green, I was made partner in 1938. I was in the Air Force in World War II and retired as a major. I became the managing partner on returning to Alexander & Green and I continued with that status for quite a while and finally I was elected senior partner. I think I was the first one that was denominated "senior partner" in our firm. That continued until I was fifty years in practice and then I became counsel.

In 1974, I was given the Award of Achievement by the Law School, which I treasure. Being number one in my class, I thought was equally important because that took in morning, afternoon, evening, downtown, and everywhere. There were four classes. Cardinal, it was either Hayes or Spellman, presided at the graduation. I went up four times for a medal and the Cardinal said "Does this get monotonous?" and I said, "Not really."

I'm the only survivor of my six brothers and sisters. I really think that four and a half years in the service helped me a great deal, physically. We were a very strong Catholic family and we didn't have any money of any consequence, but we were all reasonably decent citizens and we earned our way as we went along.

REV. EDWARD S. DUNN, s.j.

Rev. Edward S. Dunn, s.j., was the Fordham University Archivist.

My career at Fordham began in September 1933, when I arrived as a freshman. At the end of two years I entered the Society of Jesus and returned as a teaching Scholastic in July 1942, and taught at Fordham Prep for three years. I left then to go to Woodstock. I returned to Fordham in July 1977 to work full-time in the Archives and I was given the title "Archivist" in January 1978.

In the course of these 12 years, I have been able to collect a great deal of material and to process a great deal more. The Archives of the University are not as complete as they should be because we were not too careful about collecting archival material.

Today the Archives' holdings can be grouped under the general headings of Administration, Faculty, Students, and Miscellany. Administration holdings are scarce until the year 1936, but from then on they are abundant. Under the heading of Faculty, we have a complete set of Faculty Senate papers, all the faculty convocations from 1931 to date, faculty lists which include the faculty pay book from about 1950 on. I have also built up the collection, which someone else began, of the articles published by the faculty. I obtained a certain number of them through the kindness of Father Richard Doyle when he was Dean of the Graduate School.

I also have a collection of papers of some faculty members, most notably Dr. Victor Hess, who was a Nobel Prize winner in physics in 1936 for discovering cosmic rays. That was while he was in Austria. Another large collection I have are the papers of Father Harry J. Sievers, s.j., the author of the three-volume life of President Benjamin Harrison, and Dean of the Graduate School of Arts and Sciences at the time of his death in October 1977.

As for the students, we have a pretty good collection of programs; drama, oratory, sports, and music; of placards, fliers, and other forms of announcement for student activities; student publications, yearbooks, magazines, and newspapers, which are bound in the library. Recently the library had *The Ram* and *The Monthly* microfilmed and have given me the bound copies.

We have a good complete collection of Jesuit province catalogues that includes the Jesuit community from 1847, when the first Jesuits arrived at Fordham, up to date. The Archives also has a collection of photographs, some arranged by topics and topology, many others unclassified for they lack identification. We have a collection of negatives, almost 3,000, given to Fordham by a local photographer, William Fox, when he retired in 1944. He was the "official photographer" of Fordham from 1930 to 1942.

By way of summary, the Fordham Archives comprise approximately 1,500 linear feet of materials. That means that if all the boxes and filing drawers that contain our Archives were placed end to end they'd reach the length of five football fields.

There are thousands and thousands of odd items I've come to learn in the course of 12 years. I received 35 or 40 years of the Business School papers this spring. I went through them quickly—what I call "rough purge"—and 15 filing case drawers still face me. This year the Academic Vice President's office

will give me the dossiers, personnel folders, of everyone who is leaving the employ of the University. This year it happens to be about 20 or 30—they all add up.

The amount of material never ceases to come, and yet it's never enough. From Lincoln Center, for example, I get almost none of their publications, none of the fliers and announcements that I've been so careful to pick up on the Rose Hill campus and that will someday be a valuable source of material. That's the difficulty, the disadvantage of a divided campus and my inability to get down there with any regularity because even if I went there once a week I still wouldn't get all the things that are posted. Lincoln Center has no official archivist.

There are some schools of which I have no records. All I have from the College of Pharmacy, which existed from 1914 to 1974, I can hold in my two arms outstretched. They just threw stuff out when they closed the school. Everyone who moved from the Woolworth Building to 302 Broadway to Lincoln Center threw things out in the process. They would say, of course, "We don't need that." Many of them were historical records of all of these Schools.

REV. JOSEPH P. FITZPATRICK, s.j.

Rev. Joseph P. Fitzpatrick, s.j., is Professor Emeritus in Sociology. He earned his master's degree from Fordham as a Jesuit Scholastic and he taught sociology at Fordham from 1949 to 1983.

My first association with Fordham developed while I was a high school student at St. Peter's Prep in Jersey City. We used to come to Fordham for two reasons: to see the baseball games because in those days college baseball games were a major athletic event. The other reason that brought us here were the debates. We had a very active debating society at St. Peter's Prep and we used to watch for the Fordham College debates which took place in Collins Auditorium. Collins Auditorium would be filled with people from the general public. These were the early days of radio and the days before television. Public discussions took place in these college debates, and they were widely publicized and widely followed.

My next contact with Fordham was when I came here in 1937 as a Scholastic to spend one year of graduate studies in the Philosophy Department under the direction of Father George Bull, s.j. I had spoken to the Provincial about specializing in the field of social studies and social action and he told me that before I went into this field he wanted me to have a very firm grounding in philosophy. Therefore he wanted me to get a master's degree at Fordham in philosophy. I came here to start summer school in 1937 and to stay here, '37–'38, to work on my master's degree in philosophy. It was an extremely exciting time and a sense of great development permeated the Fordham campus, especially the environment of the Graduate School at that time.

The second floor north of the Administration Building had been renovated as residence rooms for the Jesuit Scholastics who were going to be pursuing master's degrees here at Fordham.

We were part of the rather impressive graduate studies program of the New York Province, which developed after a letter from the General of the Jesuits in 1934 came to the Jesuit Provincial. Father General insisted that the province become much more alert in training its members at the highest university levels. As a result many of us were sent off in the first year of our regency to do a master's program, many of us here at Fordham, many to St. Louis, and a few elsewhere, to Catholic University, for example, for science.

Ten of us, as I recall, were here at Fordham during the '37–'38 year. Father Gustav Dumas was assigned as our kind of mini-Superior. We ate with the regular Fordham Jesuit community in Loyola Hall, and of course we used the Scholastics' recreation room on one of the upper floors of Loyola Hall. Our life as Scholastics was rather restricted, especially in comparison to the situation today. We received, I think, $1 or $2 a week for carfare on the subways or buses. We used to have our own movies over in Freeman Hall. We were allowed only one or two nights during the semester at which we could go out for a dinner with the professors or the graduate students or with friends. However, it was possible to keep in contact with some of the exciting things that were going on. The *Catholic Worker* was becoming active and, although it was very controversial, it was always possible to go down to visit the *Catholic Worker*.

The liturgies left much to be desired. Looking back, if anybody thinks there have not been many improvements in liturgical life at Fordham University, they really do not know what was happening in those days. In the spring of 1938, Father Gannon decided to have the Holy Week services here on the campus. This created quite a stir of criticism and opposition within the Jesuit community. Up to that time, the liturgies were never celebrated on the campus. The members of the community could go to Our Lady of Mercy or down to St. Ignatius or one of the other parishes if they cared to do so. But I remember Father Gannon telling the Scholastics, when he asked us to prepare the liturgy in the spring of 1938, that he was always embarrassed on Holy Thursday when people would ask him where the Repository was and he would have to answer, "We do not have one on campus." He felt embarrassed about this, and in general felt embarrassed that a community as large as the Fordham Jesuit community should not have the Holy Week Services for ourselves.

I did my doctoral dissertation at Harvard on the study of the attempt to organize the white collar workers on Wall Street. It won the prize at Harvard in the spring of 1949 as the best thesis in American institutions. In October of 1948, when Father Provincial knew that I was finishing my course in November of 1948, I received a letter that read somewhat as follows:

Dear Fr. Fitzpatrick:
I am assigning you to teach soci-

ology in the Department of Political Philosophy and the Socal Sciences at Fordham University. You will report to Fordham as soon as you are fin-ished your work at Harvard, and begin your teaching in the spring of 1949. Carbon Copy to Fr. Gannon.

(signed)

JAMES FORBES

Dr. James Forbes, a 1932 graduate of Fordham College, taught in the Biology Department from 1936 until his retirement in 1979, when he became Professor Emeritus.

Biology was first offered as a course in St. John's College in 1908. Biology was first offered as an elective for seniors, 2 hours per week for the entire school year. The areas covered included Botany, Zoology, and Physiology. Biology was upgraded to 6 hours per week, 2 hours of lecture and 4 hours of laboratory. This course continued to be listed as an elective for seniors.

Rev. Gustave Caballero, s.j., was the first designated Chairman of the Biology Department. Biology was required for freshman pre-medical students and was an elective for seniors. All the sciences were taught in Science Hall, later designated Pharmacy, and later Thebaud Hall.

Early in 1926 construction was started on the Biology Building. The Department had outgrown available space in the Pharmacy building. Although the new building was to be designated Biology, it was to house general classrooms as well. The building was completed late in 1927. The cornerstone was put in place with a ceremony on October 28, 1927.

It was noted that Pius XI was gloriously reigning as Supreme Pontiff, and Patrick Cardinal Hayes, Archbishop of New York; Calvin Coolidge was the President of the United States of North America; Alfred E. Smith, Governor of the State of New York; James J. Walker, Mayor of the City of New York; Henry C. Bruckner, President of the Borough of the Bronx; Laurence J. Kelly, s.j., Provincial of the Maryland–New York Province; William J. Duane, s.j., President of Fordham University.

With the above inscription were placed the following:

New York Papers (October 28, 1927)

Catholic News (October 29, 1927)

America (October 29, 1927)

Fordham *Monthly*

The Ram

Picture of Biology Building

Current Coins

Medals of Blessed Virgin, St. Joseph, and St. Ignatius

Catalogue of Fordham University

University Enrollment for 1927–1928

Description of Biology Building

In September 1928, when I arrived on campus as a freshman B.S. candidate, all the courses were prescribed and there were no electives. For the B.S. sophomores, there was a choice of math or biology, and I elected General Biology. Father Assmuth gave the lectures, and Dr. Mullen was his assistant. Mullen arranged the class alphabetically, and the chairs were numbered consecutively. If you were not in your assigned seat when he took the attendance, you were absent.

He brought in the demonstration specimens and hung the charts for the lecture. Assmuth came in a minute or so later. When he crossed the threshold, the class arose as one! He waved us down and began talking. He was in full charge until he dismissed the class after the bell rang. He spoke with a slight German accent, but he enunciated his words clearly. Scientific words were written on the blackboard, and their roots were explained.

During the first class meeting, when the course organization was explained together with all the dos and don'ts, we were told that the class examinations were *Blitzes*, unannounced flashes of lightning, that would last 5 minutes—no more. When a blitz was planned, Assmuth entered the room, he announced "Blitz!" He took a time-clock set for 5 minutes from the pocket of his lab coat and set it on the lecture table. Mullen would uncover the paper, half-sheets of mimeograph paper, and pass out the paper along the front row to be passed back.

The questions were simple and direct. When the questions were read, the clock was started. While you were trying to put your thoughts into a lucid answer, the clock was ticking the time away! When the bell rang at the end of the time, pencils and pens were raised, and the papers were passed to the center aisle of the room. Woe to the student who tried to dot an i or cross a t! At the next lecture, or so, he would come in with a clip-board and read out the names of those who had "fallen in battle," the failures, those who had done very well, and finally the one to whom the laurel wreath was given, the one who got the top grade. Grades, however, were never given out. Assmuth said he never failed a student, he gave 100 percent to all his students, but the grade the student took was up to him!

REV. JOSEPH R. FRESE, S.J.

Rev. Joseph R. Frese, S.J., is Professor Emeritus of History. He began his Fordham teaching career as an instructor of Early American History from 1950 to 1953. He served as an Assistant Professor from 1953 to 1960 and as an Associate Professor from 1960 to 1962. Father Frese then became Fordham's Academic Vice President from 1962 to 1965 and in 1965 he served as Acting President and Vice Rector of the University. From 1977 to 1979 he was the Acting Dean of the Graduate School of Arts and Sciences and of the Fordham University Faculty. He retired in 1979.

Fordham College's Honors Program was devised by Father Thurston Davis, who was then Dean of the College. This then would be about the year 1949–1950. The idea of the Honors Program was to take three years of College students and train them in the humanities. They were selected after their freshman year on the basis of their marks and ability; and through sophomore, junior, and senior years they were given special courses in any number of fields.

Sophomore year was divided into four quarters: one for the novel, one for epics, one for poetry, and one for drama. Each quarter the students specialized in certain selected books and seminars. The seminars met every week and generally it was on Wednesdays. We would meet in the afternoon and go to dinner at a little Italian restaurant which was just under the Third Avenue El and I believe at that time we were able to get dinner for about $1.25. That would be a three- or four-course dinner. The people originally put in charge of the Honors Program were Father John Leahy, s.j., Father Victor Yanitelli, s.j., Dr. Frank Connolly, who taught English, and Dr. Lou Marks, who taught Biology.

After dinner, under the El, the sophomores and the moderator would generally go up to their room, which was on the north side second floor of Keating Hall, a little, small office, and there have their seminar. In the sophomore year, as I repeat, it was a concentration on the humanities.

In the third year, the students concentrated on philosophy, especially philosophy beyond Scholasticism; and in senior year, they were working on their major thesis, which was later defended in a public examination which was open to all students. If the student was specializing in language, his senior thesis was written in that language, such as Russian or French.

Another feature of the Honors Program at the time was that, if I'm not mistaken, there were to be four lectures a year, corresponding to the four quarters in sophomore year in the humanities. These were to be public lectures given by someone outside of Fordham University.

I was asked to associate myself with the Honors Program about the year 1950–1951. Several things were developed; there was a golden Alpha lapel pin, again developed by Rev. Thurston Davis, which was to be given to the Honors Program members. Then a medal was devised, something like a key in imitation of Phi Beta Kappa, of which Fordham was not a member at that time. This was given on graduation. Also a special degree was devised. It was recognized that Honors Program students might suffer in their grade average because they took so many extra courses and seminars. Consequently they would not generally receive the summa cum laude, because their marks could suffer somewhat. Therefore a special degree, egregia cum laude, was devised for the Honors Program students.

Another feature of the Honors Program was the Junior Year Abroad. Students were sent to Paris for their junior year of study. The idea, of course, was to get them into the universities and to let them study with French students. This proved a little too difficult and as a consequence it was decided that they would not be required to bring home a list of bureaucratic marks and courses they attended, but rather they should write three or four pertinent papers during their junior year abroad which were to be sent home and corrected here at the University. Thus they were given a full year's credit for their work without any attempt of equivalence.

It was thought at the time that equivalence was a bureaucratic or secretarial way of handling their marks, and we were more interested in their education than in their marks. We knew that the students were intelligent, capable, and what we were trying to do was interest them in studying on their own. In this connection I gave a talk at the annual meeting of the Jesuit Education Association on April 11, 1955 at Georgetown. This was later published as an article in the October 1955 *Jesuit Educational Quarterly*.

I believe that I helped run the Honors Program until 1957 when I became Superior at Spellman Hall. At that time, Bob Remini, who later went to the University of Illinois at Chicago Circle, took over until 1959 or so when I again offered to help with the Honors Program. And finally in 1962 I became Academic Vice President and was no longer able to handle the Honors Program, and Father Robert Sealy became director.

PHILIP FREUND

Dr. Philip Freund was Professor of Communications at Fordham College from 1959 to 1979.

I'd been a playwright before World War II. During my military service I was assigned to the Training Film Branch, where I became head of the board that reviewed scripts written for the troops. From that post I was invited to teach documentary script writing at City College and to lecture there in the Film Institute. At the time television was just coming in, and I was asked to write scripts for NBC. I got $35 a script, but was convinced that there ought to be a course in television film writing because it was a promising new subject. Another branch of the City College of New York agreed and hired me.

I wrote a number of letters to other colleges offering my services. I was asked by the then-head of Fordham's Communications Department, Father St. George, to come in for an interview. He said, "We've no courses in television writing; can you teach radio writing?" I had never done any radio writing, but I replied, "Yes, of course I can." I spent the summer busily preparing myself.

The Department's enrollment was rapidly shrinking. Although it had a radio station, the Administration of the University was planning to shut it down and eliminate the department.

At the end of the first year, during which I had only seven students, I told Father St. George, "There's really no point in teaching radio writing; it's a dying field. Why don't we teach television?" He said, "We've no equipment." I told him, "I can teach the subject without it; all I need is a blackboard."

The Communications Department was looked down upon as not truly academic. The highest ranking member of the department was an assistant professor, and the full-time faculty numbered only three. The others were adjuncts, like myself.

All this changed very suddenly when New York State set up a fund for distinguished visiting professorships. Fordham was given an allotment, and a Jesuit newly arrived in the Department as an adjunct, Father John Culkin, had the idea of granting this professorship for one year to Marshall McLuhan, a Canadian, who just then was earning world fame for his concept of "global village" and his popular phrase "the medium is the message." This unexpectedly attracted a very large influx of students into the Department.

McLuhan was a very abstruse speaker. It was often impossible to understand what he was talking about. Father Culkin, who was decidedly articulate, was present at all sessions of the class, and after McLuhan spoke for a few minutes, Culkin would step forward and say, "What Professor McLuhan means is this." Actually McLuhan wasn't present at too many meetings because he fell seriously ill before the term was far advanced; he underwent an operation for a brain tumor. Nevertheless he had helped to publicize Communications as a rewarding choice for students.

Another event of major impact on the Department was the Watergate scandal which involved the Nixon Administration. This caper had been unearthed and exposed by two journalists on *The Washington Post*, who received a great deal of public notice and about whose exploits a very exciting film—*All the President's Men*—had just been made. Students now saw journalism as an adventurous and fulfilling profession. Again they flooded in, so that the Department, which had been marked for extinction, over-

night became one of the largest and most popular in the University.

The Department was not called Communications then, but Communication Arts. One thing I discovered shortly after becoming a full-time faculty member was that the students knew very little about the arts. At a faculty meeting I remarked that the students' ignorance of our city's cultural treasures was deplorable. I had taken a casual poll of a class and found that not a single member had ever been to Carnegie Hall, the Metropolitan Opera, or even the Metropolitan Museum. I suggested a course giving the students some enriching background.

My colleagues thought such a survey course was a good idea and said that I should teach it. I was thinking of a course that would prepare journalists as reviewers, with some knowledge of the popular arts, a bit of technical expertise, some acquaintance of cultural history. But I was told I should include the aesthetic theories of Plato, Aristotle, Plotinus, and Maritain as well. I did all that. The course, mandatory at first, was later extended to two semesters and made elective at my request. I also introduced courses in film and creative writing, the latter—with a syllabus of seven subjects—becoming a major.

At that period, in the field of drama and literature, Absurdism was at its height. I was getting scripts which were completely incomprehensible. I thought that a good way to prove that nobody could understand them would be to have the author of one such script read it aloud in class. I had this most far-out student read his play, and I waited for the comments of the other members of the class. The piece met with universal approval, which left me quite taken aback.

The turmoil of the '60s had a very marked effect on student behavior at Fordham. There was a great deal of disorder. As has probably been mentioned by others, there were sit-ins in the President's office, and strikes and demonstrations. The trouble reached a peak about the time of final examinations in 1970, which also coincided with an unhappy incident at Kent State, where several rioting students were killed by a volley of shots from National Guardsmen.

The emotional impact of that was very strong, and at Fordham the Administration beat a steady retreat. Up to that point there had been a dress code and many rules of conduct which now were abandoned. Students were given much more input; they demanded a say about the syllabus and, in our Department, they even asked for a voice in the hiring of teachers. John Phelan, the Chairman, met this skillfully by calling a meeting explaining that the Department was about to take in new professors, but if the candidates had to undergo an interrogation or a catechism by the students, top-rate people would not apply. The students, convinced that he had a point, quickly gave way.

EDWARD P. GILLERAN, JR.

Edward P. Gilleran, Jr., is a 1947 graduate of Fordham College who was Sports Editor of The Ram *and* The Maroon. *In 1989 he was inducted into the Fordham Athletic Hall of Fame.*

In the closing years of the Roaring '20s, the Depression days of the 1930s, and the pre–World War II days of the early 1940s, college football moved into a golden age. Fordham moved right along with it. There were big names and big games, upsets and letdowns, and immortal moments that shaped Fordham's athletic history.

It was in the mid-1920s when Father Tommy Fay, Faculty Moderator of Athletics, came back from the Polo Grounds one Saturday afternoon after seeing the Fordham team humiliated once more by one of the rival Jesuit

schools. Fordham had lost nine consecutive games to Boston College, Holy Cross, and Georgetown between 1921 and 1924. Father Fay met that evening with Father William Duane, Fordham's President, and made a proposal. "If the University lent the Athletic Department $50,000 now and $50,000 more in six months, we could have a football team in three years that we could be proud of. It will be self-supporting and we will repay the loans."

After discussing the matter in detail with the Graduate Manager of Athletics, John F. Coffey, Fordham Class of 1910, Father Duane approved the program. And so it was that Fordham's golden era of football was born.

The first step was the hiring of a first-class coach. His name was Frank Cavanaugh, a legendary military officer who emerged from World War I with the nickname "The Iron Major." Cavanaugh had already carved a reputation as a football coach at Dartmouth and Boston College. Within two years of his arrival at Rose Hill in 1927, Fordham became a national power. In 1929, he had an undefeated team. In 1930, his Rams lost only once. In his last four seasons at Fordham, the last four of his illustrious life, his record was 27 wins, 4 losses, and 4 ties.

In 1930, the Associated Press ran a photo of Cavanaugh's line in newspapers across the country. The seven Ram players had allowed only one touchdown to be scored by rushing in 18 games in two seasons. The photo caption called the players "The Seven Blocks of Granite." Six years later, another set of "Seven Blocks" would become even more famous.

However, in 1932, Cav was virtually blind but he carried on, counseling more than coaching, as his assistant, William "Hiker" Joy, led the Maroon. The time had come to find a replacement for the ailing Cavanaugh. The most-sought-after coach in the country at that time was James Harold Crowley, one of the "Four Horsemen of Notre Dame." When his 1932 Michigan State Spartans won 7 and lost only 1, and beat previously undefeated Fordham, Crowley's services were in demand. Fordham acquired him, and he started at Rose Hill in 1933.

Jim's record at Fordham, 56 victories, 13 defeats, and 7 ties, including a Sugar Bowl victory in 1942, was the best in the East in his nine-year coaching tenure, and one of the four best in the nation among coaches in high-pressure situations. Crowley delivered a sparkling record despite schedules loaded week after week with the toughest intersectional powers, which came to New York primed to do their best before the New York press and public. "If you want to make All-America," "Jock" Southerland told his Pitt

players before their 1936 game with the Rams, "here is the place to do it."

Crowley and his all-Notre Dame staff developed the most famous defensive line in all of football history, the "Seven Blocks of Granite," Version Two. For three years running, this line held Pitt, the most powerful offensive team in America, scoreless. One of Crowley's assistants was Frank Leahy, destined for gridiron immortality at Notre Dame a decade later.

Father Harold Mulqueen, s.j., who spent the greater part of his life as a teacher and sports observer at Rose Hill, described the boys who played at Fordham in the 1930s and 1940s in this manner: "All of them were smart, rock-hard, and fiercely loyal. They appreciated the value of an education and performed as ably in the classroom as on the gridiron. The players learned their football from men like Cavanaugh, Crowley, Leahy, and Hugh Devore, who was later head coach at Notre Dame. They learned their ethics and cosmology from Jesuits like Ignatius Cox, Joe Murphy, Jim Kearney, and Harold Mulqueen. No wonder they all turned out so well."

What distinguished Fordham athletes of those distant days? Frank Leahy found the answer when he said, "We were a different breed in those bygone days. We played sports for the glory of our school and for personal achievement. That was all there was to it, but it was enough for us."

BERNARD GILLIGAN

Dr. Bernard Gilligan, a 1937 graduate of Fordham Prep and 1942 graduate of Fordham College, was a professor in the School of Business and the School of Education.

I was first hired at 302 Broadway in the School of Business in February 1947. In those days, students took 60 per cent liberal arts subjects and 40 per cent business. I went down at about the same time I was beginning graduate school, with only a B.A., to the Dean, Father Griffith. I had been recommended by friends on the uptown campus as I was looking for a job in philosophy.

He had none at that time, but he was sorely in need of an English teacher. He asked me if I could teach English composition and a survey course in English literature, and in my brashness of youth, I said I could. So I took a full-time job teaching those courses and, horror of horrors, a course in the writing of business letters, where I was just one page ahead of the students, although it wasn't difficult material.

In 1949, after a year and a half in the English Department, the Philosophy Department needed teachers so I was able to transfer. Dr. Joseph Sherlock was then in charge of the Department. It was rather soon after that others joined, including Astrid O'Brien and Robert O'Brien, a husband-and-wife team, and Ken Gallagher, who later moved uptown to the Graduate School.

The philosophy program then ran the gamut of Scholastic philosophy—logic, epistemology, cosmology, ontology, etc. This was long, long before Vatican II, and permission had to be gotten to read books on the Index. Teachers had to write to Cardinal Spellman, and he would give us permission for three years only to read most of the really good books in philosophy.

Around 1963 I transferred to the School of Education, partly because it had a more interesting program in philosophy. In addition to the Scholastic system, they had history of philosophy courses. Father Joseph Hassett, who later left the Order, was the Chairman of the Department. Dan Sullivan, who unfortunately died a few years ago, was a very well-known individual there and a very charming person.

When I first arrived as a student in the Graduate School in 1947, it was very much on the verge of change. We had people teaching there like Dietrich von Hildebrand, who was a pupil of Husserl's, the founder of phenomenology. We also had the famous Dr. Robert Pollock, who was a great historian of philosophy and in whose classes you'd come out swimming with a thousand insights. He was very, very free in his thinking. I guess you could say that both of them were anti-Thomists. I was fortunate enough to attend the School when the program in philosophy was beginning to open up and get away from the strictly systematic, Thomistic approach.

Pollock saw things in thinkers that most other people would have never discerned at all and saw continuities between modern and medieval philosophers. Both he and von Hildebrand would interest you in a way that you knew this is where you were going to stay for the rest of your life. I took any and all courses I could with them. I did my master's dissertation with von Hildebrand on the phenomenological method, and Pollock was the second reader. And I did my Ph.D. dissertation on philosophy and psychiatry with von Hildebrand and again Pollock was the second reader. Graduate school in philosophy was one of the most wonderful experiences of my life.

Another individual who had a tremendous influence on me at Fordham College was Father William Lynch. He taught Greek, but he went way beyond that. He was just an extraordinary person, who had profound psychological insights and was extremely helpful to those of us having typical as well as atypical adolescent difficulties. He later became editor of *Thought* magazine and also taught in the Graduate School. He and I became very fast friends, and in many ways I think I owe my sanity to Father Lynch.

REV. WILLIAM M. A. GRIMALDI, S.J.

Rev. William M. A. Grimaldi, Professor Emeritus, starts his oral history of the Classics Department in 1959 and ends it in 1988, the years plus one, 1949–1950, in which he was a member of the Classics faculty. The account reflects his recollections of faculty, students, academic programs, and events during this time. For want of all and any departmental records, the chronicle is precisely that—a personal recollection based on memory and his notes.

The faculty of 1959 opens his account, and as he moves along he marks the arrivals and departures of departmental faculty. Academic programs at the graduate and undergraduate level as well as the quality and number of students over the course of the years are mentioned. In the early years the presence of the Graduate De-

partment in the Carter Report, unique among Catholic and most public and private universities, and the successful acquisition of two NDEA programs are discussed. Since it was as a member of the Classics Department that he was the founder and director of the Honors Program of Fordham University's college for women, Thomas More, he speaks at some length of that program.

Academic requirements such as Fordham's "language" requirement and the "experimental" curriculum revision of the '70s, the 4–4 program, receive attention insofar as they affected the Classics Department. In the course of his account, events such as the annual Horace Academy, dramatic readings of Greek and Roman plays with the cooperation of the Mimes and Mummers, the relations of the Department with the short-lived Bensalem College and the Jesuit Scholasticate at Shrub Oak, the Core Curriculum revision of 1979—all are noted. The chronicle ends with the spring semester of 1988. The '80s are somewhat briefly recounted not because the author ran out of steam but because the present Classics faculty are well able to fill in any lacunae.

In 1962 with the encouragement of the Classics Department, the Latin–Greek requirement for a Fordham College A.B. was dropped. The retention, however, of the language requirement as a "Modern Language" and not a "Foreign Language" requirement resulted in a significant injustice to the students of Latin and Greek. This continued for seven years in Fordham College but Thomas More College removed the problem within two years after its inception by specifying the requirement as a "Foreign Language."

Foreseeing uncertainty surrounding the revival of Latin and Greek in the years ahead, I did a study (Fordham Alumni Magazine, Winter 1963) of the Honors List of the recently graduated classes of 1961 and 1962; the latter class was the first recipient of our new Phi Beta Kappa chapter. The results were interesting. Two of our three Rhodes Scholars were Latin/Greek students; one of them, in fact, a classics major. These men were chosen from the highly competitive Northeastern section of the United States. Our two Danforth Scholars did Classical Languages as did our two Fulbright Fellows who went to Spain and France. Ten out of 13 Woodrow Wilson National Fellowships were Latin/Greek students as were two of the three who won West German Government Fellowships. Our Classical Languages students won 31 of Fordham College's 57 New York State Regents Fellowships. Twenty of the 30 graduates of the Fordham College Honors Program were students of the Clas-

sical Languages as were 15 of the 30 selected for Phi Beta Kappa in the Class of 1962.

I averaged this out statistically, and since no one ever challenged the figures, I took it to mean that they were correct or that no one had read the article. Classical Languages graduates were statistically 25 per cent of both classes. This small group garnered 47 per cent of the total fellowship awards which came to Fordham College, 50 per cent of the Phi Beta Kappa awards in 1962, 56 per cent of the New York State Regents Fellowships, and 75 per cent of the Wilson Fellowships, and constituted 66 per cent of those who graduated in the Fordham College Honors Program, or in the official designation which they, at least, would understand: In Cursu Honorum.

In brief, as we see from the years 1959–1988 the competence and quality of the Department and its faculty is to be found in evidence like the foregoing. It is also found in other testaments like the Carter Report, the success of both its applications (its only such) for two NDEA programs, the publications (both journal and book) of the faculty, the presence on the faculty of the Editors of *Traditio*, and of *The Classical World*, the Secretary of the American Philological Association, a MacArthur Fellow, along with which there were three competitive fellowships for a year of study at the American School for Classical Studies in

Greece won by its graduate students, as well as summer scholarships at the American Academy in Rome won by others. But the moment comes to call a halt to this ". . . tendentes opaco Pelion imposuisse Olympo."

REV. JAMES E. HENNESSY, S.J.

Rev. James E. Hennessy, S.J., began his Fordham teaching career as an instructor in Greek and Latin in Fordham College from 1945 to 1949. He was the Director of the Guidance Office of the College from 1949 to 1953 and he served as an Assistant Professor of Theology from 1953 until 1964.

The Counseling Center, Previously Known as the Educational Guidance Office of Fordham College

A bit of history helps to explain the origins of the Counseling Center. In the years immediately after World War II, our colleges were besieged by many veterans who wanted very much to get a college education along with the usual high school graduates. So it was a time of some turmoil. We didn't have enough room to accommodate all who applied to us.

At this time, many colleges were starting guidance offices. It the late '40s; it was the "in" thing to do. As we'd say today, it was the state of the art. In the summer of 1949 there was a Guidance Institute at Fordham. All 28 Jesuit colleges and universities of the American Assistancy cooperated and participated in this institute. About 150 Jesuits from all parts of the United States took part.

Father James Moynihan of the Society of Jesus, an eminent psychologist from Boston College, was the director. He recruited experts, both Jesuit and lay, to address the participants on the various functions of such an office. I recall very well after the six-week summer institute just about everybody pronounced it a great success and the men returned to their colleges all enthusiastic about starting a guidance office.

At Fordham, the Dean of the College, Father Thurston Davis, and the assistant dean, Father Eugene Culhane, invited me to a follow-up conference. There I was told that the President at the time, Father Laurence J. McGinley, wanted me to start this new service for our students. This was two weeks before the semester was to begin. At the time I was also adviser to freshmen, and one of the duties of that position was to run the orientation program for freshmen and to administer the various tests that were given. So from this vantage point I was able to explain to our new students what the Guidance Office was all about. But first I had to learn what it was all about.

The Guidance Office was designed to serve all the students in Fordham College, but it was especially pointed toward the freshmen and sophomores, and in each of these years, the freshmen and sophomore class had 500 students each. As freshman adviser, I got to know the faculty, both Jesuit and lay, very well. I wrote a letter to them explaining what we planned to do. Forty of them volunteered to help. These were experienced educators who recognized that college students often needed help with study problems and vocational choices, as well as personal financial difficulties and many other areas that come up normally in college life. We had several conferences to prepare these 40 faculty members to be counselors to our students.

In practice, each freshman and sophomore had a counselor. Each of the 40 faculty counselors had 20 to 25 students assigned to them and they met once a quarter or more frequently. They had the grades of the students before them, and their problems would be discussed. If needed, referrals would be made either to the Guidance Office or to the student counselors or the various deans. In some rather exceptional cases referrals were made to psychologists or psychiatrists for further inquiry and testing.

My underlying philosophy in running the guidance program was that it would be a help to every student who entered Fordham College to have an older, experienced man in whom he could confide, come to in any difficulty because college kids have all kinds of difficulties. It's a great change in their lives. Many of them are away from home and they're confused. So, to have an older person to whom they could go and really put their trust in his judgment and find the counselor would not be judgmental, but helpful. It didn't always happen, and in later years I think they changed the philosophy.

Of the special projects we undertook, one that I remember with great affection was for sophomores because at that time at the College you did not make your selection of a major until the end of sophomore year. It was a big decision, of course, for all students. So that in preparation for this choice we had normally about 20 lectures to which we invited all sophomores—and many freshmen came as well. We had experts in various fields and professions, including a lawyer, engineer, psychiatrist, medical doctor, banker, and so on. We also had representatives of the professional fields such as English, the Classics, and Mathematics.

REV. THOMAS C. HENNESSY, S.J.

Rev. Thomas C. Hennessy, S.J., began his long association with Fordham in 1941 as a Jesuit Scholastic assigned to teach at Fordham Prep. From 1951 to 1961 he served as student counselor at the Prep, and he was then assigned (as happened those days) to the University's School of Education. There he spent 20 years in the Counselor Education Program. He was Director of the Kelly Counseling Laboratory from 1969 to 1981 and coordinator of the Counselor Education Program from 1975 to 1979. He left Fordham for the four years between 1981 and 1985 to serve as Dean of the School of Education at Marquette University.

Regency at Fordham was a great time for learning, not only about young boys, but also about teaching. In my years in schools of education, I would tell prospec-tive teachers about the experience of those years. There would be about a dozen Jesuits in this same capacity, namely, teaching high school, living together, working together, and recreating together. In many ways it was a fabulous way of sharing one's experiences, learning what works and what does not work. I moderated a Debating Society; I ran the Fordham Prep Book Store; and I initiated an organization which, I believe, is still going on with a slightly different name called the Gaelic Culture Society.

In my second tour of duty at the Prep, the guidance counselor was assigned to be a military chaplain, and the principal asked me to be the Student Counselor. Before actually taking on the job, I visited all the Jesuit high schools in the neighborhood and spent a day with the counselors there to find out what precisely they were doing.

In general the counselors were interested in the vocational and educational plans of the students and the places they would go for advanced training. An additional main concern of the Counselor at that time was students' religious development. So I tried to follow the example of other counselors in the area, recognizing that the personal choices and interests of each student whom I studied were very important.

Counseling at Fordham Prep and Fordham College was always a strong religious activity. Counselors typically taught religion classes in senior year and took care of religious activities and multiple services around the school. When I became Student Counselor, there was a broadening of interests, not only at Fordham Prep, but at other Jesuit high schools and in education in general. This broadening included making the counselor's job a full-time professional one. It was an important element of our stance as counselors that we should not also be teaching.

One of the usual things at that time, that we don't see any longer, was devotions to the Blessed Mother in the month of May. Each class day we had a talk given by one of the seniors on one of the titles of the Blessed Mother, and all the students assembled outside in Edwards Parade where there was a statue of the Blessed Virgin. On rainy days it would be held indoors in the Old Prep, Hughes Hall.

One project I was anxious to have completed was a chapel in the Prep building. It was built on the third floor. Al Smith, who was the main carpenter on the campus at that time, I'm sure, exercised very special care in the carpentry work in the Chapel. We had a special day of dedication, and Father McGinley, President of the University, was there and gave a brief talk. I recall that Father McGinley noticed tears in the eyes of Al Smith at the mention of his name for being so

helpful in the construction of the Chapel.

When I moved to the University, much of my work was done downtown at 302 Broadway. When Fordham decided to build the Lincoln Center campus, there was a great deal of activity and discussion as to what we should ask for in the new building. I made a specific plan for a counseling laboratory. Others said, "Let's wait and see what they offer us." I disagreed. My plan included audio and video facilities and a demonstration conference room, connected to a classroom, where we could have a two-way mirror arrangement.

My plan, at first, seemed to go for naught when I learned it had been integrated with the plan of another department. However, after making some objections, we found that the plan was reinstated, and eventually Father Philip Dobson, who was in charge of planning at the time, introduced me to the architects. I noticed that Father Dobson gave a hardly visible nod to the architect, and that meant the plan would go through. I was also very happy that we were able to run a small campaign among alumni to get the counseling laboratory dedicated to Dr. William Kelly, who was the mentor of my dissertation and also the Director of Graduate Studies at the time and who died shortly before the building was constructed. So we have the Dr. William A. Kelly Counseling Laboratory on the tenth floor of the Lowenstein Building.

My main concern about Fordham is that it seems more and more to be losing its tradition of religious commitment. I would regard my work at Fordham as undermined, useless, and all quite in vain if Fordham lost its identity as a religiously oriented institution. It doesn't have to be religious in the sense that it was in the 1840s. Development is a natural and a good thing, but there are some signs that make it seem we are developing along ways that many of the Ivy League schools developed. That I would lament. The present situation looks good to me, but there are signs of decay. Let's hope that our progress in religious lines accompanies progress along other lines, such as academics.

REV. WILLIAM T. HOGAN, s.j.

Rev. William T. Hogan, S.J., joined Fordham's Economics Department briefly for a year, 1950–1951, before leaving to complete his theology studies. He returned permanently in 1956 and has been a professor of Economics at Fordham ever since.

"The Steel Priest."

My interest in steel began with the doctoral thesis I did in the late 1940s on productivity in the steel industry. At that time not too much had been done on this subject, and my thesis required that I get some information that was not generally public.

I talked with some people at the United States Steel Corporation who had not been particularly free with handing out information other than the annual report and literature that was published for general consumption. I went out to Pittsburgh and spent three hours discussing this question with the vice president of engineering, a man by the name of Lawrence. At one point he said to me, "Well, I don't know if we can go along with you because if we do it will cost us a lot of time and some money and effort and I just don't know why we should."

I figured if I was going to make it, I was going to make it in the next five to ten minutes, so I very enthusiastically explained what I was going to do and how I thought it would be a benefit to the economy and he sat back and listened and agreed to go along. I spent a year in Pittsburgh and was able to get access to information on costs and man-hour production that had never been published before. As a result, I finished the thesis in one year. Mr. Lawrence, at the end of my year out there, asked me to come back and spend another year to study the industry a little more broadly, which I was able to do.

In the middle of that year, U. S. Steel was preparing a study on guaranteed annual wages, which they expected to be a bargaining issue in the next go-round with the union. The study had bogged down somewhat, and Mr. John Stevens, who was the chief of labor negotiations for the industry, asked me if I would take the direction of it because they wanted an outside person. It was not popular with everybody there, but they recognized that was what they wanted. I completed the study in about two and a half years and by that time I had become knowledgeable in the whole steel industry. So in getting involved to that extent, I then decided I would write a history of the steel industry over a one hundred year period from its beginning.

When this history of the steel industry started out, I thought it would be possibly two volumes. But it just kept expanding because in developing the history of the steel industry it was necessary to develop a history of the industries that are steel consumers, including the railroads, the automotive industry, and oil and gas. It grew to five volumes, covering the period from 1860 to 1970 and was published in 1971.

After that I became interested in the world steel industry as well. As a result, in the early 1980s I wrote a book entitled *World Steel in the 1980s, A Case of Survival*. Then I became interested in just what the steel companies in the United States were doing to meet the competitive force that the Western Europeans and Japan had mustered. A number of American companies felt the influx very seriously, so I decided to write a book called *The Steel Industry in the United States, Restructuring to Compete*. Other nations had to rebuild their steel industry after World War II, and they did so with new technology.

Our industry wasn't touched by bombs, so, for a period, we made some of our steel in the equipment that we used during the war, but realized we had to modernize a significant part of our facilities.

Then came the institution of the mini-mill, which is a small steel operation that uses an electronic furnace and does not involve itself with the heavy blast furnace and coke ovens necessary to the integrated company. The mini-mill has really carved a niche for itself in the U. S. steel industry, and so in 1987, I published a book comparing the mini-mills with the integrated mills.

I'm in the process now of writing a book entitled "Global Steel in the 1990s, Growth or Decline?" because a lot of people in the industry feel they don't need any more capacity while the Third World feels it needs a lot more capacity to take care of its own needs. There is no question that they need more steel, but whether they have the purchasing power to turn that need into effective demand is a question.

For the past two years, the Steel Company of India, which is the largest steel company in India, has sent over nine middle management people to Fordham and asked me to conduct a course to broaden their knowledge of the steel industry. We usually have them here for five or six weeks. I give some of the lectures myself, but have brought in quite a number of experts in various aspects of the steel industry, from production to sales to technology. I've been delighted to do that and have enjoyed it very much.

IRMA B. JAFFE

Dr. Irma B. Jaffe, Professor of Art History at Fordham (emeritus since 1988) was invited to join the faculty in 1966 with the special task of setting up a Fine Arts Department. She chaired the new department until 1978.

My spiritual and intellectual debt to Fordham is very great. One of my happiest memories is standing on the terrace of Keating Hall for the first time, looking over Edwards Parade and feeling enchanted by the scene. The campus looked glorious on that beautiful spring day. Some of the Jesuits, dressed in their traditional habits, were strolling along the walks in the shadow of the leafy trees, and I felt transported back to the Middle Ages. The peaceful serenity of the atmosphere, the Gothic Revival architecture, ap-

pealed to my sense of the romantic, even the exotic, and also expressed the kind of intellectual commitment that attracted me compellingly. It was really love at first sight. I decided on the impulse of the moment that I wanted to leave my Research Curatorship at the Whitney Museum and apply for a faculty position at Fordham.

I did not know there was no art department at Fordham. I sent my résumé to the non-existent Art Department, and fortunately it came into the hands of Father John Donohue. He had been appointed Dean of the newly founded Thomas More College for Women. He and his assistant, Dr. Patricia Plante, had decided to include art history in the curriculum of the new college, and my letter found a welcome. I was invited for an interview and a few days later I was no longer in the museum world, but had begun a new career in academia, as Chair of the Fine Arts Department, with a faculty of two—myself and Dr. James Kurtz, appointed at the same time as a musicologist.

It was a heady experience, starting a new department. With the strong support of Father George McMahon, Dean of Fordham College, Father Donohue, and Dr. Plante, we were able to offer a major in art history in our third year, with three art historians added to our faculty and a respectable slide collection, starting with zero slides.

In those early years we were educating not only our students but also the Jesuits. Once the great art patrons of Europe, the Jesuits after the Suppression had little interest in art, and very few took art history seriously. Then in 1969 I organized the symposium "Baroque Art and the Jesuit Contribution," and my Jesuit colleagues were impressed, particularly because of the world-famous intellectuals who participated, Rudolf Wittkower and Francis Haskell among them. The beautiful volume of the proceedings produced by Fordham University Press (and now a much-sought-after classic in the field) made us all proud.

The Jesuits again revised upward their estimation of art history when I became the first Fordham faculty person to win a National Endowment for the Humanities Fellowship to work on my John Trumbull book, which came about through my colleague Dr. Andrew Myers. He was preparing to chair a meeting of the Modern Languages Association and asked me to take a look at the Trumbull drawings in our library's special collections and give a talk about them at his meeting. The library had the drawings restored, and they are now famous as Fordham treasures, constantly requested for loans all over the country.

The year 1969 was one of financial crisis. As it happened, I had just organized a faculty club with promised support from Father Timothy Healy, Executive Vice President. Then it turned out the University was in financial straits, and all programs had to be curtailed or eliminated. We managed to have our faculty club opening party, however, which Roger Wines called "On the Rocks," and kept the club going for a few years with faculty support. More important, this crisis occurred when I was organizing the Baroque/Jesuit symposium. Father Healy had to withdraw the University's promise of financial support, but we managed to get funding from the American Council of Learned Societies, the Kress Foundation, and private gifts. In the end we had money left over, which I added to my "Schulman Legacy" fund.

Jacob Schulman, a Connecticut man, liked my book on Trumbull—the Trumbulls were Connecticut V.I.P.'s—and bequeathed $10,000 to our Department. Every year I buy fine prints with the income, and we now have an excellent collection. A few years ago my senior seminar students created a catalogue of the collection as their semester project. How hard they worked! And how proud they—and I—were, holding the published catalogue in our hands.

One of my ongoing intellectual interests has been in the links between American and Italian art. My first book was on Joseph Stella, published by Harvard

University Press in 1970 and republished by Fordham University Press in 1988. Since retiring from teaching I have been associated with the Italian Encyclopedia Institute and have brought the I.E.I. into association with Fordham in a series of symposia on "The Italian Presence in American Art." When the series is completed (symposium III is scheduled for November 1991), three beautiful volumes of the proceedings will have been co-published by Fordham University Press and I.E.I.

Fordham has benefited in an unusual way from my book on the sculptor Leonard Baskin. Since he was pleased with it, I asked for a favor—would he make a bronze relief of a ram, as a gift to Fordham? He did, and we now make casts from the original plaster, to give as gifts to our very special benefactors.

The Honors Program that I initiated in 1970 stands out in my mind as a favorite academic achievement, and for extracurricular activities, certainly my greatest experience was the Bread-and-Soup-of-the-World Undinner, which I organized in 1982. For over a year students, faculty, administration, and staff worked on this hunger banquet, with essay contests on world hunger, seminars, and then the evening itself, with Senator Bill Bradley of New Jersey heading the speakers, and Helen Hayes as the star of the three-hour entertainment extravaganza. An exhausting, wonderful event.

"I have a dream." I'd like to see Fordham lead a campaign to dig a tunnel under Fordham Road from Southern Boulevard to Third Avenue and transform Fordham Road itself into a beautiful garden-type shopping mall, with a good motel, good places to eat, and a Center for Performing Arts right at our corner of Southern Blvd. and Fordham Road. It would revitalize this area of the Bronx, and thus enhance Fordham's image as one of the most desirable universities in the country. That's my dream—my hope. As Emily Dickinson wrote, "Hope is the thing with feathers / that perches in the soul / And sings the tune without the words / and never stops at all." I guess I'll always hear that silent song of hope for the best, for Fordham.

REV. WALTER C. JASKIEVICZ, s.j.

Rev. Walter C. Jaskievicz, S.J., was the Director of the Institute of Contemporary Russian Studies from 1952 to 1969. He was also the founder and Director of the Language Laboratory from 1960 to 1969. From 1952 to 1986 he was an assistant and associate professor of Russian. Since 1978 he has served as the Associate Director of Alumni Relations.

The Institute of Contemporary Russian Studies

At its beginning, the Institute caused quite a bit of furor and, at the same time, confusion. Two institutions were established about 1950 at Fordham, two Centers of Russian Studies. Long before 1950 a group of Jesuits led by Father Frederick Wilcock, s.j., an English Jesuit, had adopted the Byzantine (Eastern or Russian) Rite in order to be better able to work among Russian-speaking peoples. They had spent some time in Harbin, China, taking care of Russian refugees who had fled the Soviets. When that colony began to disperse, the Jesuits eventually found their way to New York and wished to establish an apostolic center here. After much deliberation and search, Fordham University gave them a building at the east end of Coffey Field. Barracks built during World War II to house trainees were remodeled for them.

When I arrived in 1952, Mulcahy Hall was already redone and an Eastern Rite cupola had been added over the door leading to the small chapel. By then the building had been renamed Soloviev Hall, in honor of the Russian theologian, philosopher, and mystic Vladimir Soloviev. He became, more or less, the house patron. Several of the Eastern Rite Jesuits were living there at this time, and a few were scattered in various colonies in the United States and Germany.

It was about this time, and possibly related, that Father Thurston Davis, then Dean of Fordham College, thought it a good idea to establish an academic center of Russian Studies. During World War II, interest in anti-Communism and knowledge of the Soviet Union were in short supply. After the war, interest became high.

Unfortunately, among the Jesuits, none was academically prepared to organize such a program. Thus Father Davis began collaborating with Father J. Franklin Ewing, s.j., who came to Fordham after release and recovery from internment in the Philippines. Father Ewing, because of his mission interest, emphasized the value of the various cultural aspects or what came to be known as "area studies."

So the "academic" and "apostolic" were integrated in the planning stages. Father Davis invited his classmate from Fordham, Dr. Richard Burgi of Yale University, to come to Fordham on leave from Yale for a year to organize the Institute. In 1952 the Institute became associated with the Graduate School, and a graduate program was elaborated. It confused many people because the Institute was not exactly a separate department within the School, nor was it a school by itself. My first assignment on arrival in 1952 was to straighten out the program and get rid of some unacceptable accretions adhering to the Institute.

Our Russian Language Program was expensive, but good. A result of the teacher-language/informant program was that the Institute came to be substantially aided by monies appropriated by the National Defense Education Act. In any case, our reputation was being spread far and wide.

Perhaps the Soviets themselves helped. When the Institute was first announced, the Soviets lampooned Fordham's efforts to start a "spy school." We used this cartoon, which I happened to notice in *Ogonyok*, a Soviet humor magazine. It pictured the "typical professor" in cap and gown instructing the typical student, who was unshaven with close cropped hair and with a cigarette dangling from the side of his mouth. Grenades, pistols, and knives protruded from various parts of his clothing as he watched the professor trace the trajectory of a bomb falling on a factory. A cute verse mentioned that Fordham had inaugurated a spy school in 1950 and it was not flourishing. Even Moscow paid attention in those days.

The "research activities" of the Institute were funded by the Army Map Service and the Central Intelligence Agency. They were unrelated projects, but they did utilize the skills that we developed here. We were able, by accepting these projects, not only to do work for the two government agencies but also to give students practical training in the use of the language while supporting them financially. This was hardly a "subversive activity," an accusation made against us when the CIA was in disfavor.

In the 1960s, a financial crisis hit the University. One of the "economies" proposed was to phase out the Institute. It was too costly. The dispute between the Institute and the Administration went on for some time. It was really surprising to review the

Ram articles where people were being accused of being insensitive to world problems, of taking away the opportunity of learning, of neglecting area studies programs to the detriment of the nation, and other prophetic utterances.

In 1969 the Institute was dissolved to be incorporated into Modern Languages. Out of a faculty of 16 in various fields in its heyday, the Russian wing of Modern languages now has two people, one in language and linguistics, the other in literature. I regret that we missed the opportunity of developing the Institute into a real ideological center of research on the influence and spread of atheism in the Soviet Union and the world at large. We predicted the weakening of Soviet and Marxist ideology in 75 years; it is happening. We needed a bit more publicity of the right kind.

Shortly after the demise of the Institute, the John XXIIIrd Center for Eastern Christian Studies (originally the Russian Center) was transferred to the University of Scranton in Pennsylvania.

REV. JOSEPH G. KEEGAN, S.J.

Rev. Joseph G. Keegan, S.J., joined the faculty of the Psychology Department in 1942 and served there until 1974. He was Chairman of the Department from 1949 to 1958 and he served as Director of the Counseling Center from 1961 to 1966.

At the time I came, the department already consisted of two divisions, graduate and undergraduate. I was engaged in the undergraduate as well as in some graduate courses. In general, I think our department anticipated the rest of the University in having teachers who were responsible for teaching at both undergraduate and graduate levels.

What also distinguished the Psychology Department was that it started not in the College, but downtown in the Woolworth Building at the graduate level. So instead of the usual procedure of graduate work growing out of the interest of the college faculty, we established a graduate program downtown which, after moving to Rose Hill, offered courses in the College. And for a while, the only psychology that was empirical would be taught in the classrooms and laboratories at the Woolworth Building.

The whole program was disrupted by World War II. Dr. Robert T. Rock, who had been Chairman, Dr. Lawrence T. Dayhaw, Dr. Edward Monahan, and Dr. Thomas Snee just floated out into military service. The government snatched experts, specialists in what we would call psychological techniques, because much propaganda was made of how the Germans had been preparing for years for psychological warfare. That was the expression employed, and there may have been some effort on their part to develop a military psychology. I guess our government felt we had to be prepared for this and ready with an answer.

Dayhaw was a Canadian and he was called back into the Canadian army and he never returned to Fordham. Tom Snee was called to our Army's Department of the Judge Advocate. He also had a law degree, so when he returned to Fordham after the War, he went to the Law School and taught there instead of returning to the Psychology Department.

We were also faced with a great

reduction in the number of male students. That was certainly notable in the graduate level, as the number of women students was disproportionately increased. I also remember teaching an undergraduate course in 1943 that had 79 juniors, about 50 of whom were enlisted in what they called the enlisted reserve. They were all called up one day in May, and we had about 25 students left in a large classroom.

The Counseling Center was started after Father Bill Bier succeeded me as Chairman of the Psychology Department. We were all aware of the need of some kind of formal organization for counseling. There had been a Guidance Office on campus in Dealy Hall back in the '50s directed by Father James Hennessy. The University thought it would be more relevant if it were related to the Psychology Department. Dr. Alexander Schneiders was brought on from Detroit to set up the whole operation. He stayed for about five years, but he left Fordham to join the psychology staff at Boston College. That was when I was asked to be in charge. And it was at this point that the Placement Office became a separate operation from the Counseling Center. I continued to teach, but with a reduced program.

I was associated with many outstanding people in the Psychology Department over the years. One was Dr. Joe Kubis, who contributed so much through his steady devotion, his feeling of closeness, and his intimate relationship with all his colleagues at Fordham. He was a graduate of St. John's College in Brooklyn, but in his thoughts and attitudes he always felt himself to be a part of Fordham. He could serve as a fine role model as teacher and researcher, a person with whom you could raise problems and discuss solutions.

The other person I considered among my top people in terms of influence would be Anne Anastasi. She has been a great inspiration and help to our students. Any student who worked with her must inevitably have absorbed that same spirit of dedication to academic and professional ideals. Considering the fact that Fordham is not as distinguished a university as Stanford, Yale, or Harvard, it is somewhat surprising yet very rewarding to know that she could become president of the American Psychological Association.

REV. NICHOLAS J. LANGENFELD

Rev. Nicholas J. Langenfeld, priest of the Green Bay Diocese, Wisconsin, is Professor Emeritus of the Fordham University Graduate School of Social Service. He taught in the School of Social Service from 1934 to 1967.

My earliest recollections of Fordham University go back to 1932 when I met Father Edward S. Pouthier, s.j., at the University of Louvain. He was then the Assistant Dean of Fordham University Graduate School of Sociology and Social Service since 1929. We both enrolled in the Ecole des Sciences Politiques et Sociales, and we became close friends. To prepare ourselves for the final ten oral examinations on a single day, we took long walks in the countryside and fired questions at one another.

When we finished our course, he invited me to teach at Fordham. I came to New York City in January 1934, to get acquainted with Fordham University and New York City, my home for the last fifty-five years.

I gave a course, "Social Work and Religion," in the evening school in the fall of 1934. The evening sessions were conducted by Dr. Edward L. Curran. Nearly all public transportation converged at the Woolworth Building, which led to a very large evening attendance. After a few weeks, my course in "Social Work and Religion" caught on, and Father Pouthier elevated the course to the full-time day schedule. He made me Research Director and, given my heavy teaching load, I soon forgot to finish my Louvain doctoral dissertation. I enjoyed teaching.

About one-half of our classroom was lined with blackboards, which suited my teaching style as a chalk-talker. I also wrote a 72-page research manual. The common room was used by both faculty and students and fostered much informal socializing. More sophisticated socializing occurred in the Postskeller, named after the old Post Office in City Hall Park. After the success of my course in "Social Work and Religion," Father Pouthier asked me to teach an additional two courses: "The Family" and "Social Research."

We had very many nuns and

quite a few priests from Catholic Charities. They were my best students. I had them pick a research topic that dealt with their Order. In the case of priests, they usually wrote histories of the Catholic Charities to which they would return after graduation.

Incidentally, in my course in "Social Work and Religion," I attracted many people from the Jewish agencies, Salvation Army, and the Church Mission of Help (Episcopalian). My best students in the course were Jews—rabbis and sons and daughters of rabbis. They really relished the course because they didn't have any similar course in the Jewish School of Social Work in New York City.

I was deeply impressed by one blind student, Mr. Paul Sauerland, who was totally blind. Despite this great handicap, he got the Alumni Medal as the best student in the two-year curriculum. Another prominent student was Bishop Francis Mugavero of Brooklyn. I had charge of his research. Monsignor Andrew P. Landi was another brilliant student. He was in command of the Catholic War Relief Services— N.C.W.C.

Many of my students became teachers in our School. Seventy-five per cent of our faculty at one time were my former students. Among these were three of the Deans of our School: Dean James Fogarty, Dean Rita McGuire, and now our present Dean, Mary Ann Quaranta. Four Philippino bishops were my students. A

Mother General of the Missionary Servants of the Most Holy Trinity was my student. James Norris, the only layman to address Vatican II, was my student. Thirty-four of my students became directors of diocesan charities. Monsignor James Murray of New York Catholic Charities is a shining example. The Archduchess Charlotte, sister of my Louvain classmate the Archduke Otto, was my special student. I mentored her master's dissertation.

The most interesting group I ever had was the police quartet, consisting of officers Ralph DeMayo, Al Olsen, Helen Block, and Regina Flynn. When they came to class with their uniforms and their side arms, the discipline was perfect. Ralph DeMayo took the roll call and barked out the names as top sergeant. He woke up the class for me. He was no respecter of a person—instead of calling out "Sister Mary Grace McCarthy" Ralph simply called out "McCarthy"; Right Rev. Monsignor Joseph A. Tapia was called out "Tapia."

In all, I taught about 2,000 students in three different courses, and I mentored about 1,100 masters's dissertations.

In celebration of my many years at Fordham, I donated the equivalent of a million dollars, in addition to my house. My house was appraised at around a half million dollars. I donated stocks and bonds to Fordham. I have a saying, "The money you give during your lifetime is golden. What you give in your will is silver." What you give in your lifetime, you give with a warm hand.

Since we restarted the doctoral program and since research is one of the hallmarks of graduate stud-ies, I made my million-dollar do-nation in the hope that the funds would be funneled into the re-search department of our Gradu-ate School of Social Service. The "Langenfeld Research Center" within the Graduate School, is really built around the Chair.

FELIX E. LARKIN

Felix E. Larkin, class of 1931 at Fordham College, was Chairman of Fordham University's Board of Trustees from 1970 to 1977. He headed the search committee which recommended Rev. James Finlay to succeed Rev. Michael Walsh as President of Fordham.

When Mike Walsh decided in 1972 he had to go back to Boston College, he was not feeling too well. I think he had a heart condition. A little one. But I guess he was here two or three years through tough times and he decided he had to go home. So he got a hold of me one day and said, "Felix, I've got to resign and go back to Boston." I said, "Oh, Mike, don't do that; we just got things going here." But he said he had to go, and since he was such a wonderful man, we accepted his judgment.

So then we had to find a new President. There was a majority of laymen on the board. I concluded that it was absolutely critical that the new President of Fordham be a Jesuit. I was a layman as the Chairman, and I could help with the Board in the commercial aspects of the University, but I had no ability to help in the scholastic {aspects} and the curriculum and so forth; that was the role of the Jesuits in my opinion. I felt so very strongly that we had to have a Jesuit President that I made myself the chairman of the search committee to ensure that that would happen.

But it was the first search committee for a President that had members of the Board of Trustees, a few of them, members of the faculty, students, members of the alumni, so it was kind of a polyglot group. I wrote a lot of material which I delivered to this committee at the first meeting and I got them to adopt it right on hand. I wasn't going to have them write the rules and regulations. In the meantime, I had written to all the 28 Jesuit colleges in the United States and asked them if they would recommend any Jesuit as a candidate for President. I received 60 nominations. I did this before I called the first meeting. I got everything done, and a lot of them wrote back and said they weren't interested. Meanwhile, Father John Padberg finally came on our Board.

He looked like a good candidate but he wouldn't take the job. Then, I solicited résumés from all the nominees, and when I had the first meeting and I said we have to have a Jesuit, well, there was a big push. Why have a Jesuit? This is an open University now, and why not have qualified laymen? Well, I wouldn't stand for that so what I did was kind of a sneaky thing. I called up the man who was the president of Columbia at the time, William (Bill) McGill.

He was a Fordham graduate. I knew him very well. I said, I'm looking for a new President of Fordham and you're a distinguished educator, the president of Columbia. Would you be interested? He said, "Oh, for heaven's sake, no. You want a Jesuit." So I was able to say I solicited a couple of laymen and they wouldn't consider it. We finally eliminated people who wanted to be eliminated and came down to about five candidates. Among them was Jim Finlay, who was then the Dean of the Graduate School of Arts and Sciences here and had been at Fordham most of his educational life.

Don Monan, who was on the Fordham Board, but was a Professor of Philosophy at Le Moyne at the time, was one of the five. It came down to two candidates, Father Monan and Father Finlay, and we brought them before the Board, and we asked them both their view of what Fordham

needs. Those two presentations were the most brilliant presentations I ever heard. They were wonderful. They had the Board of Trustees on its head. They couldn't pick between them. We had a vote all day. We had six votes. It was like electing the Pope. We couldn't get a two-thirds majority for either one of them.

I said to Mike Walsh, the University President, "Gee, Mike, I don't know how we're gonna get a majority; five-eighths is necessary." Mike said, "Well, we have to keep at it." He told me he had first voted for Father Finlay and the next time he voted for Father Monan. I said, "What did you do that for? You're messing the whole thing up." "No, no," he said, "I just want to keep it alive." Well, anyway, it finally came out, and we picked Father Finlay and I had to call Father Monan and tell him that after six votes we settled on Father Finlay. Father Monan said, "Jim's a wonderful guy; I'm so delighted." He was just so great.

And I went to see Father Finlay about five o'clock that night to tell him the news. I couldn't find him. I later caught up with him. I said, "Where were you? You've been elected President." He said, "Oh my heavens. I was over at the hospital visiting my secretary, who is sick." I said, "There you go."

REV. J. QUENTIN LAUER, S.J.

Rev. J. Quentin Lauer, S.J., was a professor of Philosophy at Fordham from 1954 to 1990. During his entire teaching career, Father Lauer lived in Martyrs Court as a Faculty-in-Residence.

During the 35 years I've been teaching, I've lived in the student dormitories in Martyrs Court, which makes me the oldest living inhabitant. When I initially came here in 1954, the title that I had was Prefect. I never quite figured out what Prefect meant, but that was the title, and on each floor of each building in Martyrs Court there was a Prefect. All of them were Jesuits, by the way, and we were expected to, you might say, really keep a very close eye on everything that was going on in the dormitory.

It was expected, demanded really, that all students be in by 11:00 at night, at least on weekdays, and everyone of them on my floor had to come in and report to me. Then I had to check off that they had come in to see me. Obnoxious in some ways, but in another way, I look back and wish that we had something like it still. Every single night I saw every single student, and I got to know them, which is not true today.

After the term Prefect and then "Chaplain" were given up, the role was turned into "Faculty-in-Residence," and that is still the title that I have. I think the reason for the change was that as Prefect and as Chaplain there was some connotation of authority in those titles. Faculty-in-Residence carries with it very little connotation of authority. You're there just to be consulted if they feel like doing that, and actually I have to take the initiative most of the time, even if it's only to go in and sit and talk with them. They don't come to me, except if they have academic problems or if they want to borrow money.

When I first came here, the undergraduate Philosophy Department was entirely Jesuit. There were those who said I should be thrown out because I did not teach a strictly Thomistic brand of philosophy.

What I did do was to teach philosophy from an historical point of view. I would tell them a great deal about St. Thomas

Aquinas and let them see that he was an extraordinarily great mind, but not the authority that you have to follow in every single instance. In other words, yes, historically, a very great mind, but you don't have to be Thomist if you don't want to be, and by that time I wasn't one either, even though I probably knew more about St. Thomas than most of the people teaching here.

I just did not believe in authoritarian philosophy. It's ridiculous, a contradiction in terms, and gradually other professors started doing the same thing, having them read not only the ancient philosophers and the medieval philosophers, but the modern philosophers, and come to the realization that they had to be exposed to a lot more than they had been exposed to before.

The President of the University—this is way back—one night after dinner, said, "Would you like to take a walk?" During the walk he said there were some complaints about the way I was teaching undergraduate philosophy. So I said, well if you want me to go out to a parish, I'll go, but if you want me to stay here, I have to teach it my way. Well, the fact that I had a doctorate from the University of Paris precluded their wanting to fire me. But it ended up, no problem. Nobody complains about the way I teach philosophy anymore.

In the 1950s, students were better equipped than they are now. I don't mean more intelligent, but more geared, especially linguistically, grammatically, to handle what they were studying. Just read the student newspaper, *The Ram*, and *The Monthly*, in the '40s and '50s and see how much better written they were than they are now. The grammar was better, the spelling was better, the thinking was more cogent. I think they were trained in high school better than they are now.

HONORABLE LOUIS J. LEFKOWITZ

Photo by Bachrach

Louis J. Lefkowitz was a 1925 graduate of Fordham Law School who went on to be New York State Attorney General from 1957 through 1978.

Law school at night was extremely difficult. I got up early in the morning. I had to be at the office at nine o'clock. The office was located at 15 Park Row, right across the street from the Law School. I often did without my dinner at night. I worked till about a quarter to six and ran across the street to make the evening session. Then, I went to the automat at 15 Park Row. Dinner consisted of a sandwich and a cup of coffee. I didn't get home until midnight.

I was a law clerk. It was invaluable to be a law clerk. I learned

so much. It made my studying a lot easier. Plus, I was not a graduate of college. Most of the students were graduates of college. Very few students were high school graduates. I was too young to go to law school, and I had to wait a year and a half for admission. I graduated from high school when I was sixteen and a half. Then I had to wait to take the bar exam until I was twenty-one.

I was a big shot. I received $5 a week. I had two employers: one was Jacob Kirschenbaum; the other was Herman Kahn. When I told them I could type, they said, "You type, and we'll give you $3 more in salary. . . ." That gave me $8 as a law clerk/stenographer. I took Gregg shorthand, which I learned at the High School of Commerce.

The shorthand was a big help in law school or I couldn't keep up with my notes. No one else could read my notes. When summertime came I continued to work at the law firm. I read some cases there and I developed a fondness for the law, an appreciation. . . . I urge any law student to become a law clerk. I'm a firm believer in getting a year or two of clerkship, which is something you don't get in law school.

I went to law school Monday through Friday. I was a youngster then, just barely eighteen. It was tough, but if you got by the first year you were all right. About 90 per cent in my class were college graduates, most from Fordham at Rose Hill. We had a good class, very active at Fordham. Charles E. Murphy was our class president, a great man.

Headed by Murphy, our class president, the Tortfeasors Club was famous. The teachers came to a dinner, which was held once a year. It was a great party, just great. It was pretty well attended by almost everybody in our class. The class kept it up after graduation, but the club died out as people got older.

One of the things I remember best was the good comradeship. I knew several fellows in the first-year class, but 99 per cent of the class I did not know at all. I was of the Jewish faith. Most of the class was of the Catholic faith. No one ever asked what your faith was, which I'll say is to Fordham's credit. It was Catholic-oriented. The teaching was excellent; the comradeship was wonderful. No incident in the school ever made me feel uncomfortable.

I lived in a tenement building, a cold-water flat, with my mother and father, brother, and sister—432 East Houston Street.

I was proud of Fordham University. They gave me my start in life. I always refer to Fordham wherever I go. I gave many students from Fordham Law School a position in my office when I served as Attorney General.

As a young lawyer, I was not doing very much. I had very few clients. I joined the local Republican club. In those days, there was the high tariff and the low tariff, which was the difference between the Democrat and Republican parties at that time. In a district of a thousand people, I canvassed, knocking on every door, asking for their vote.

I lived in the 6th Assembly District in Manhattan, which had about 20,000 registrants. I personally canvassed as many votes as I could and had all my friends help me out. Because my opponent was an incumbent assemblyman for six years, no one gave me a chance of winning. I was shocked when I was elected. The headline in the newspaper said, "Eastside Republican Wins." That's how I started. The term of office in those days was one year.

From the day I won, I had to campaign for the next year. When I was elected, Alfred E. Smith was the Governor. He was a good friend of my county chairman, Samuel S. Koenig. Governor Smith sent for me one day and teasingly said to me, "Were you the young man who was elected on the East Side as a Republican?" With mock sternness on his face, he said to me. "Don't ever get elected again as a Republican." When I appeared upset, he said to me, "I'm only fooling."

A. PAUL LEVACK

Dr. A. Paul Levack began his long association with Fordham as an Instructor in the History Department of the Graduate School of Arts and Sciences in 1936. He attained the rank of Assistant Professor in 1942 and that of Associate Professor in 1947. He was Chairman of the Department from 1950 to 1965, became a full Professor in 1967, and served as Dean of the Summer Session from 1965 to 1978. He has been Professor Emeritus since 1979.

In the spring of 1936, when I was a teaching fellow at Amherst College on a one-year appointment, I received a letter one morning from Father Lawrence Walsh, Dean of the Graduate School of Arts and Sciences at Fordham, telling me that I had been recommended to him by Father Robert Lord, formerly of the History Department at Harvard, and inquiring would I be interested in coming to Fordham for an interview. I was quite interested, but a few days later I received another letter, this one from Harvard, stating that I had a grant for next year to study in France and work on my doctoral dissertation.

When I asked the people at Harvard as to what I should do, the mentor of my dissertation told me that I should certainly go to France, forget the job, and finish my thesis. When I next spoke to Professor McIlwain, the best teacher I ever had, he said, "Look, jobs are scarce these days. . . . I think it would be a good idea for you to go down there . . . and start teaching." I decided to follow his advice, and came down here to the Woolworth Building where the Graduate School was located.

Here I met the Dean, Father Walsh, and members of the History Department faculty. They explained to me that though the graduate courses in the natural sciences were taught uptown at the University's Rose Hill campus, all the courses in the humanities and the social sciences were taught in the Woolworth Building. More important to me was that they offered me a contract and sketched the sort of program of courses I would teach in the fall semester. My salary, incidentally, was to be $2,100 a year—which in those days was considered a very fine starting salary. Then I went home to Boston, spent some of the summer in the Harvard Library, and came to Fordham in September.

At the first faculty meeting I attended, we were greeted by Father Robert Gannon, who had just been appointed President. He told us he had great things in mind for the Graduate School. He intended to move all of the School that was in Woolworth Building to Keating Hall, a new building just being finished at Rose Hill, where we would have a much better library.

As the move was gradual, with a few courses being offered in the fall and a few more in the spring, I had the opportunity to observe some of the School's principal features downtown. All courses were scheduled at 4:15 in the afternoon or on Saturday mornings, principally because most of the students were teachers or teachers-in-training in secondary schools, intent upon getting a master's degree or in some instances just course credits in subjects they were teaching. This is what seemed to be the main purpose of the Graduate School. The faculty, it seemed to me, was a very good one generally, and some of its members were of exceptionally superior quality. The facilities they had for counseling and study and for conferring among themselves, however, were inferior. So too were the library resources.

Now Father Gannon made it clear that he had a different sort of school in mind. He hoped to have day courses, full-time students, some of them would become resident students on campus or nearby off-campus. Especially he hoped and planned for a faculty more interested in promoting and directing doctoral studies with, of course, many more students in the departmental doctoral programs. Among his objectives, moreover, was a closer association of the Graduate School with Fordham College.

What is remarkable is the extent to which some of these objectives were realized, first in the years 1938–1941 through the celebration of the University's Centenary, and then in the years immediately following the Second World War. It was in the first of these years that so many distinguished scholars and scientists, both Americans and Europeans, joined the Graduate School faculty. What was most noticeable after the war was the increase in the number of full-time students in doctoral programs, largely because of the faculty that attracted them here—just as it was the location of the entire Graduate School on the University's main campus that had attracted several of that faculty to Fordham. The major consequence of these developments was the improvement of Fordham's reputation as an institition for advanced studies.

The extension of the influence of the Graduate School upon

Fordham College in those years, however, was not great. Although some seniors in the College were encouraged to take introductory graduate courses, and a few members of the Graduate faculty were engaged to offer courses in the College, the two faculties remained distinctly separate until the administration of Father Laurence McGinley, who succeeded Father Gannon in 1949.

Early in 1951, when I had been chairman of the Graduate School's Department of History for only a few months, I was notified that Father McGinley had decided to integrate the two faculties to form a single Liberal Arts Faculty on Rose Hill. When he called me to his office to discuss this arrangement, Father McGinley told me that the merger would be departmental, with the Graduate chairmen to be the chairmen of the new single departments and the College chairmen becoming the assistant chairmen.

While the majority in both faculties appeared to be pleased with, and some of them enthusiastic about, the decision to integrate, there were two unfavorable reactions to it. In the Graduate School there were some people who felt a graduate school and its faculty should not be contaminated by association with undergraduates, that graduate study was something altogether different, and that it prospered best when the faculty who were engaged in it were engaged in nothing else. Then there were those in the College who felt it was they who would be contaminated, that in the integrated departments the graduate faculty would be pushing the ideas of graduate study upon them.

When we integrated, what I had was an altogether new association with Fordham University. I became more interested in undergraduate students, in understanding their objectives . . . and in counseling some of them to go on to graduate studies. That again is something to notice: how few Fordham College students prior to this went on to graduate study in the arts and sciences and a teaching career in higher education. Now we began to have students who applied for graduate fellowships . . . and within a few years the number of Woodrow Wilson Fellows . . . and Danforth Scholars . . . and even a couple of Rhodes Scholars that we had was amazing. I think a good deal of this was partly the result of the impact of Graduate faculty upon the undergraduates. . . . As for me, . . . though the Graduate School was still my first attachment, I found my greatest satisfaction at Fordham in the College.

Then I was sort of demoted. I became Dean of the Summer Session. There I had great success owing to the wonderful cooperation of the faculty in all of the University's schools and colleges, and to the genius of Father

Charles O'Neill, who founded
the university-wide Summer Session in 1963.

LUCY K. LOUGHREY

Lucy K. Loughrey, who earned her master's degree from Fordham's School of Social Service in 1951, was Admissions Director of the School from 1959 to 1976. She taught Social Welfare Policy in the School from 1953 until her retirement in 1980, when she became Professor Emeritus.

When I entered Fordham's Graduate School of Social Service in 1947, I was a work/study student on leave of absence from the Department of Welfare. At that time I was already a supervisor and I had passed the Case Supervisor's exam. There were quite a number of students going to the various schools of social work in the metropolitan area and, although we didn't get a grant of money, we got a stipend for one year.

The work schedule was ad-justed. Also I took many of the courses in the evening. Of course, I met a lot of students there who were doing the same thing, from some other agencies besides the Department of Welfare, and some of them were on their own.

Actually, when Fordham School of Social Service was founded in 1916, it was as a result of the vision of a group of men who were corrections officers, and who recognized the need. Their clients were working class at that time and new immigrants, who got into trouble. These corrections officers realized that the people needed help to keep out of jail, as well as help while they were in jail. Of course, it's important to realize that these clients at that time were mostly Irish, Italian, and German people recently arrived in New York City.

Now these corrections officers had an awful lot of difficulty getting any organization help then. They went to Fordham University and spoke to "the powers that be" there in 1916, and they helped them by accepting the School of Social Service as a part of the University, including housing. As a result of the foresight of this group of officers, the Catholic Charities of the Archdiocese, the parish St. Vincent de Paul Societies, and the New York City Department of Corrections joined together to form the Fordham University School of Social Service. I believe it was the first such school in the United States under the auspices of a university.

In 1953, I was appointed an assistant professor and assigned the Public Welfare sequence. One of the highlights of my experience came in 1966, when there was a very large Convocation at Fordham in honor of the then General of the Order (the Jesuits call their top director "General"), Father Pedro Arrupe. The main speech was by the rather famous Jesuit orator Father John Courtney Murray, and it was about the period from 1960, of Vatican II, and this was 1966, and that speech of Father Courtney Murray's was very much ahead of its time.

Some of the problems he mentioned were racial. There would be turmoil and chaos and people taking sides and interpreting the new rules to suit themselves. I was teaching Social Welfare at the time. I felt that I should have the students introduced to the Encyclicals because there were social programs outlined and there were labor programs: *Rerum Novarum*, The Condition of Labor, in 1891, and then forty years later, it was the *Quadragesimo Anno*, 1931—both of these had to do with social living and labor problems—and then the up-to-date ones, of course, were two, *Mater et Magistra* in 1961, and *Pacem in Terris* in 1963.

It was the School of Social Service that first decided the need to do research on and offer a course in racism. Dean Petraglia, Dean

Tricomi, Rita McDonnell, Dr. Patricia Morisey, and I team-taught. One contribution Rita made to the Institutional Racism Curriculum was based on her experience growing up in the Bronx in the 1930s. At that time, there were "unofficial" Irish, Italian, and German parishes in the Bronx and other Boroughs of New York City. Perhaps unwittingly, they set the stage for geographical segregation in the future. This historical perspective helped students understand how institutions and systems have always impacted on the lives of families and children.

During the 1960s and 1970s, or going back to the 1950s, when we were at 39th Street, in a separate building, we were much more isolated from the general University. Fordham had sponsored this school and helped its development from the very beginning, in 1916. However, as time went on and financial problems developed during the Depression, it is true that individual Presidents and committees on "the campus," as we called it, would be looking to see where they could cut back. I don't think they saw us in the same light as they saw the Law School. Even now, in 1989, as I speak, I'm inclined to say "we" and "they." I think this reflects our own feelings and the people we serve.

Helen Dermody and Gilda Petraglia received the Bene Merenti medal at the same time as I did, since the three of us came to

Fordham in the same year. The narrative in the Convocation program of Sunday, October 21, 1973, stated, among other items, "Professor Loughrey received her early education in her native city of Belfast. It was undoubtedly in that land where the art of letters is so revered that she acquired the proficiency and grace of language." It was there that I experienced the problems of religious persecution and ethnic problems as a child. The Bene Merenti committee brought out that they felt that this experience helped my "awareness and sensitivity to the problems of minority group students," and that as Admissions Director I was very conscious of Fordham's interest in the black and Puerto Rican students and applicants and that I helped to recruit and finance them.

JOSEPH F. X. McCARTHY

Dr. Joseph F. X. McCarthy, Professor Emeritus in the Graduate School of Education, was Fordham's Academic Vice President from 1976 to 1984. He earned his master's degree from the School of Education in 1950 and his doctorate in history from the Graduate School of Arts and Sciences in 1959. During his tenure as Academic Vice President, Dr. McCarthy was involved in several new programs to expand the University's reach, including the branch campus at Tarrytown.

Most colleges and universities in New York State have had branch campuses of one sort or another. Fordham, during the 1930s and '40s, had a branch campus in Stamford, Connecticut. We had branches at several of the motherhouses of religious sisters and, at some of those branches, we offered programs for lay students in the area.

During the 1970s it became evident that there was a very large number of potential graduate students for the professional schools who were associated with businesses, schools, or agencies in Westchester and Rockland counties. In an effort to retain Fordham's presence in those professions, Fordham sought, and eventually found, a suitable branch campus at Marymount College in Tarrytown.

The arrangement required us to promise that we wouldn't offer undergraduate work there. That was Marymount's operation, and they of course announced they wouldn't offer graduate work. Three of our professional schools—Graduate Business, Graduate Education, and Graduate Social Service—agreed to open branch campuses at Tarrytown.

The difference between a branch campus and an extension center is important both in law and in operation. An extension center is some place where you offer a course, or possibly two or three courses. A branch campus is a place where you offer a degree program. In order to offer and support degree programs at Tarrytown, we promised, and in fact it was my job to see that we delivered on the promise, to allot full-time faculty at the campus, suitable library facilities, and to ensure that students at that branch campus would be fully equal to those at our Lincoln Center campus, the original home of all three of these graduate schools.

For several years, in the 1980s, the Graduate School of Education operated a branch campus in Puerto Rico. That came about initially because of legislation in Puerto Rico that mandated that every teacher in a special education program had to complete a program of 12 to 20 academic hours in suitable preparation. The only problem was that the Legislature did not provide funding for such programs by the institutions then in Puerto Rico. Fordham, among others, was invited to offer such courses. We did, and the courses were popular enough with the Puerto Rican teachers that we were subsequently invited to offer a doctoral program in curriculum and teaching in Puerto Rico. We did that, and we arranged for a three-summer presence of those students in our Lincoln Center campus. That was an interesting experiment.

One other very interesting development was the creation of the Third Age Center, the Gerontology Center, operating now at Lincoln Center. In origin, this flowed from my belief that there was a field, gerontology, in which Fordham was not then playing a very prominent role, although the field was growing and, I thought, full of promise.

So I kicked this off with a University-wide meeting to which people were invited from each college or school of the University and from each department. Bob Senkier, the Dean of Business, was especially interested in the Gerontology Center because of the impact of retirement plans and of retirement financing on business organizations. Mary Ann Quaranta, Dean of the School of Social Service, saw this as an area in which Social Service should play a dominant role. But other departments had an interest in it. Psychology, as one example, Sociology, and even the Department of Spanish showed an interest in it because of possible language services.

It attracted the benevolent interest of George Doty and his wife, Marie. He was just leaving as Chairman of the Board of Trustees when he and his wife made a handsome contribution which enabled the Center to operate on a firm institutional basis in addition to whatever funding could be generated from public and private foundations, and on the basis of tuition developed within the studies on gerontology.

JOSEPH W. McGOVERN

Joseph W. McGovern is a 1933 graduate of Fordham Law School. He also served as a Professor at the Law School from 1936 to 1966 and as a Regent of the University of the State of New York from 1961 to 1975 and as Chancellor of the University from 1968 to 1975.

I graduated from Fordham College in the worst year, I think, that anyone could get out of college, 1930. The big boom had gone bust and we were headed for the biggest depression this country has ever known. I got a job teaching at Regis High School in Manhattan, my alma mater, so I could go to night law school.

On a typical day, I started teaching at nine in the morning down at 84th Street and I would usually be through no later than 2:30 in the afternoon. I would go

home to where I lived, near Fordham at Rose Hill, and I would use whatever time I had before dinner to do school work, and then I walked over to the campus. Classes began uptown at 6:30 P.M. My weekends were spent doing a lot of my law school work. My tuition each year was $200.

The Law School had two divisions at that time, one in the Woolworth Building, the downtown division, and the uptown division was on the College campus, in the Biology Building, on Fordham Road. You could walk into the building from the Fordham Road sidewalk without having to go through the campus. The Law School had three classrooms there. There was a little office out of which whatever business was necessary was conducted, and we had a modest law library located in the College library close by. That was it.

The Night Registrar was a man named Frank Delaney. He took attendance, answered any questions. I believe he taught at Fordham Prep during the day. The Dean came up once a year to give out the prizes and occasionally he was a pinch-hitter for a professor who was ill.

I don't think there was ever a competitive spirit. There was a different atmosphere on campus, especially in the springtime—the trees were in bloom, very different from the atmosphere in the Woolworth Building. But we had very fine students. Three of my classmates in that uptown section became professors at the Law School. In addition to myself, there was Joe Doran, who became a judge as well, and Bill White. We didn't lose more than ten per cent of our class over three years—and we didn't lose them through flunking out. Mostly we lost them due to their full-time job requirements or relocation of their places of employment.

We had some wonderful teachers. John F. X. Finn, who taught New York Practice, was dramatic. Dramatic! He had all these fictitious characters that he'd weave into his teaching. Also, there was Walter Kennedy, who was the first person in charge of the *Law Review* when it was started. I remember the great George Bacon, so dedicated to the Law School, and we had Bill Meagher, too. He was one of the founders of Skadden, Arps, Slate, Meagher & Flom. And then there was a fellow we used to call "Doc," Doc Roberts. He was a very high official in the Board of Education, City of New York, and he'd always sit down at the desk and throw out his arms, and you'd see his white cuffs and cuff-links. A great gentleman. Very precise. He taught Evidence and taught it well.

My salary for my first year of teaching at the Law School in 1936 was $3,000. Remember, the big problem was in getting a job after law school in 1933. Number one question, "Could you get a job at all?" and number two, "Would you be paid maybe $15 a week?" I was first in my class, and I was happily surprised. I started at $25 a week. I got a job with Vincent Leibell, later a federal District Court Judge, who spoke at my commencement in 1933. That was the twenty-fifth anniversary of the first Law School commencement and he was a member of the first graduating class.

I had a tough decision to make when Dean Wilkinson asked me to join the faculty. I had three years of practice under my belt and I was doing quite well for those years. I was all the way up to $50 a week and that was good, real good. I thought I could teach well because I had teaching experience, so I made a career resolution. I said to myself, "I will do this for five years, and I will do my damn'dest to do as good a job as I am capable of and at the end of five years I'll make a decision to stay teaching or return to private practice. I did return to practice after teaching nearly seven years full-time and continued part-time until 1966, when the pressure of my work on the Board of Regents forced me, reluctantly, to take a leave of absence.

Bill Mulligan was one of my students. I watched him grow up around the corner from me in the Bronx. I strongly recommended him for Dean. He was teaching at the time in the Law School and doing an excellent job, very highly thought of. One of the objections to him as Dean was "He's so young." I remember writing to Father Laurence McGinley, who was then President of Fordham, saying, "Look, don't listen to anybody who says he's too young because Dean Wilkinson was younger than Bill Mulligan when he became Dean."

DENIS McINERNEY

Denis McInerney is a 1948 graduate of Fordham College (originally Class of '45) and a 1951 graduate of the Law School, cum laude. He served as President of the Law School Alumni Association from 1968 to 1972 and was the principal attorney for the Fordham Jesuit Community in its incorporation in 1968. McInerney is a partner in the New York firm of Cahill, Gordon & Reindel.

Fordham Law School after World War II

When I arrived at Rose Hill, I was still in my paratroop uniform and wearing my boots. That went on for the first few weeks because there was a real shortage of men's civilian clothing. The war had ended sooner than expected due to the atom bomb, and no one had any inventory. It was very difficult to get good threads, as they say today. Having come back from a pretty bombed-out Europe, the campus looked great to me. Everyone was quite friendly, either because they had shared the same experience, or because they were interested in what had happened. It was very easy to locate a group in the cafeteria that would be a congenial group.

We took all our classes in the same room throughout law school. It didn't occur to us that this was, in comparison to what the students now have, some kind of deprivation because we had no basis for comparison. There was a lot of camaraderie in the group. We used to go out and have a few drinks together after classes—and certainly after exams, when you'd have two factions, one group that wanted to rehash the test questions and the other that would get a headache just thinking about that. I was sort of a rehash-the-questions type at first, but I found it didn't do much good since there were essay questions mostly and you'd have as many answers as you had people.

I was the class president throughout law school. I was rumored to give good parties. That was my principal function, as far as I could tell. I used to try to do that at least at the end of the year, a dinner dance in May or June, right after exams when everybody was feeling kind of let down and in need of a lift. There was no place at 302 Broadway to do such things, so we had them at the Fifth Avenue Hotel and similar places. There was also a bar on Chambers Street, a kind of subway bar—you went downstairs. We used to congregate there after classes or after exams. We used to call it just "Chambers." We thought it had a legal ring to it—"See you in Chambers."

Incorporating the Jesuits

It came about as a result of two very different convocations. One was the Second Vatican Council which ended in 1965 and preached greater ecumenism and more lay participation in the life of the Church. The other convocation was called the Bundy Commission after its head, McGeorge Bundy, who was appointed by Governor Rockefeller to study the possibility of state aid to private and parochial schools. The Bundy Commission recommended state aid to the extent legally permissible. Some Catholic colleges did make drastic changes to obtain needed state aid. Fordham, of course, didn't do that, although it too was anxious to qualify. However, in an effort to have a broader base of leadership and because of the opportunity for state funds, in 1968, Fordham, for the first time, chose a Board of Trustees having a majority of laymen.

Shortly after that, the Jesuits of Fordham were incorporated. It was not paranoid to wonder whether some future lay board at Fordham might decide that the University had better uses for Loyola Hall and Faber Hall than housing Jesuits. In the same vein, at that time the Jesuits had their living expenses paid by the University, but they did not get salaries, or the pension and other fringe benefits the lay faculty received. That too could pose a future problem.

The Jesuit residences at Rose Hill and a small vacation or retreat house known as Mitchell Farm were transferred to JO-FINC, or Jesuits of Fordham, Incorporated. The University agreed that these properties really belonged to the Jesuits who had more than paid for them. Also, JOFINC entered an agreement with the University to provide Jesuit faculty as required and be paid what lay faculty would be paid. Individual Jesuits receive pension benefits, and JOFINC takes care of expenses of the community and its members, contributing the remainder to Fordham or a similar charity. The Jesuits who live at Fordham are under their rector's authority as Jesuits, but under the authority of the University as faculty. So JO-FINC was not really created to get some additional state aid. It was more a matter of assuring the Jesuits of what was rightfully theirs. I believe it also, perhaps for the first time, showed the University in a dramatic way the value of the contributed services of the Jesuits.

JOHN J. MACISCO, JR.

Dr. John J. Macisco, Jr., who earned his B.A. from Fordham College in 1958 and his M.A. from the Graduate School of Arts and Sciences in 1959, began his Fordham teaching career in 1960 as an Instructor of Sociology. He returned to alma mater in 1972 after a Ph.D. from Brown University. He had been Associate Professor of Sociology at Georgetown and Program Specialist with the Ford Foundation in Chile. In 1975 he was appointed Professor and from 1986 to 1989 he served as Chairman of the Sociology Department and head of the University Research Council.

As a kid growing up in the Bronx, Fordham was up on the mountain. You had no conception of where it was. It was a place that most of us aspired to go to. It was away, but you knew it might be available to you. A good fifteen kids in my neighborhood went to Fordham.

Fordham was, in a sense, the pinnacle of higher education for us Catholic boys because at that time we were not allowed to go from a Catholic grammar school, and then a Catholic high school, to a non-Catholic college. I forget the exact canon, but it was read to us. It was a major shift, as you well know, when the boys from Regis, Fordham Prep, Rice, and Power—namely, the feeder schools—were allowed to apply to the Ivys.

In a sophomore class, Introduction to Sociology with the late Father Joe Scheuer, C.S.S.P., who showed me the tremendous power that sociology had for explaining the socioeconomic situation, I grew very quickly from high school (Rice High School, Irish Christian brothers, 124th and Lenox Avenue in Manhattan) to Fordham College, where the world opened up intellectually.

I was privileged to be at Fordham in the three years that Tom O'Dea was there, namely, my junior year, my senior year, and my first year of graduate school. Tom had a way of making the workaday be illuminated through hard science, soft science, through historical method. I don't know what you want to call it but it made sense; it worked.

He came to Fordham largely because Fordham was supposed to offer a place where he could do sociology, but it would have as a formal object the role of the Catholic church in American society. Father Joseph Fitzpatrick, s.j., was pulling a team together to do that. Prior to Tom's coming, Frank Santopolo, Joseph Schuyler, s.j., and Joe Scheuer were here. Joe Scheuer started what we would call "parish" sociology, which took demography and human ecology and related it to, in this particular instance, the Bronx.

Frank Santopolo taught the Basic Methods course; Joe Scheuer taught Urban Sociology courses, but, again, using human ecology and the frame of parish sociology as the analytic frame. Joe Schuyler was just finishing his book on a Northern parish, which was Our Lady of Refuge, after the Joe Fichter, s.j., tradition of Southern parish.

So Fordham was exciting. Scheuer, Santopolo, and Schuyler were just finishing their Ph.D.s in the Department of Sociology, and they brought a kind of raw empiricism to bear on the theoretical works of people like Nicholas Timasheff and Tom O'Dea. It was an exciting place to be. I stayed for my master's degree and then was fortunate enough to be asked to work another year as an instructor in sociology, under Leo McLaughlin, then Dean of the College.

In 1961 the Department of Political Philosophy and the Social Sciences voted to split into three departments: Political Science,

Sociology–Anthropology, and Economics.

I think Sociology was at the edge of having more students and wanted to get some autonomy. We were then sharing one secretary, part-time, for some 15 people. There were people like Friedrich Baerwald and Timasheff, distinguished scholars, there. I shared an office with Timasheff, Bill Gibbons, s.j., and Joe Scheuer. In the next office were Fitzpatrick, Rosemeyer, and John Martin. We had one phone, and it had to be passed between the offices.

In any case, the separation was done, and it was the beginning of some very powerful times for Sociology because the Jesuit Order had decided that seniors somewhere along the way had to have a course in social ethics. The Sociology Department volunteered for that. I left for Brown before that occurred but they were gearing up for it. Paul Reiss was brought in, and they had classes of 350 over there in Keating One. The seniors rebelled because they didn't want this new demand that was placed on them in senior year. But Joe Fitzpatrick ran with that and was able to hire a lot more faculty as a result.

I think the generosity among the faculty to the students is still there, but the form has changed somewhat. Now why do I say that? I guess it's because the prevalence of a three-day week has become central to a lot of people's thinking. The pressures to publish for tenure have necessitated this three-day week. People are not in their offices the way it used to be when I was an undergraduate. You would walk in and see faculty in Silk and King-O'Neill halls. The doors were always open.

When I was here, there were Jesuits all over the place, and not in mufti either. I think the fact of a residential community of scholars was a fact that enabled students to have access to more of the faculty. That has changed, and I think that mitigates against the availability of faculty. However, a generous spirit still persists. And with the advent of more faculty research with student involvement, the future looks promising.

REV. GEORGE J. McMAHON, s.j.

Rev. George J. McMahon, s.j., was Dean of Fordham College from 1962 to 1974 and Vice President for Administration from 1974 to 1987. Since 1987 he has been Vice President of the Lincoln Center campus. Father McMahon earned his M.A. in Philosophy from Fordham in 1949.

In June of 1962 I had been Assistant Dean of St. Peter's College and working with Leo Mc-Laughlin, who was then Dean of St. Peter's. One morning I woke up and learned that I was to be Dean of Fordham College beginning July 2nd. I had not even the slightest suspicion that I was to be Dean. I was to remain Dean until June of 1974.

Without placing them in order of importance or chronologically, let me list those events, people, programs, structures that most readily come to mind.

My Assistant Dean, Father Charles Loughran, was a genius at picking out of the Freshman Class the Woodrow Wilson Fellowship winners of four years later.

The relationship between the Dean of the College and the Dean of the Graduate School of Arts and Sciences. There was no Dean of Liberal Arts faculty. We divided the Departments between us.

The beginning of Thomas More College in 1964 when I worked closely with John Donohue, s.j., the first Dean.

The student organizations and activities which reported to me and for which I was responsible—the concerts, including the Kingston Trio and Peter, Paul, and Mary; the return of football to Fordham; the reorganization of the curriculum by vote of the faculty from a five-course program to a four-course program. It was probably the first time the faculty voted on the full curriculum. My relationship with senior faculty, real gentlemen and real scholars who had a better idea than I of what Fordham was all about and who were most kind, indeed respectful of me. Professors like Levack, Partlan, Frasca, O'Sullivan, Liegey, Walsh, Cronin, Donahue, Vial, Connelly. I know I am forgetting some.

The workings of the Dean's office, which was really the hub of the College since everything went through the office, including exams, blue books, vouchers, etc. The result was that the best-known person on campus to both students and faculty was my secretary, Stella Moundas.

The total involvement of the Dean's office in freshman orientation. The senior gowns worn by all seniors—kind of a love-hate relationship. The 125th Anniversary celebration. The faculty and staff dinner at the Astor. The light and sound on Edwards. The financial problems of 1968 and the consequent student unrest—their Blue Army.

The Vietnam War protests which grew year by year, reaching a climax in the spring of 1970. It began with one student in 1966.

The emergence of the African American students as a force on campus. The beginning of the Afro-American Institute and courses in Afro-American history. The beginning of Bensalem College, the experimental college which had a number of difficulties, much discussion, and some excellent alumni.

The beginning of the Rose Hill Council and its demise in 1973.

The fire in the Campus Center and the arrangements for final exams.

The effect of President John Kennedy's assassination on the campus and the Mass at Commencement for Robert Kennedy.

The student protests concerning tenure decisions. The takeover of the Administration Building.

The beginning of the HEOP program in 1968. Still going strong.

The Mexican programs and outreach programs of the '60s before they became a national phenomenon.

The various Assistant Deans who worked in my office, three of whom are now college presidents.

The Fordham Club through which the Deans came to know the student leaders of each class.

The constant search for space, the renovation of Dealy Hall, Collins Hall, Faculty Memorial Hall, Thebaud Hall. The construction of Mulcahy Hall and the Lombardi Center.

The successful efforts finally to keep Rose Hill green. The merger of Thomas More College and Fordham College in 1974.

The cultural events and speakers on campus: Salvador Dali, Itzhak Perlman, Madame Nu, Mayor John V. Lindsay, Senator Kenneth Keating, Bobby Kennedy, William F. Buckley, Jr., Helen Hayes, Colleen Dewhurst, Edouard Villella.

Encaenia, faculty holding their breath as they listened to the Lord of the Manor and Valedictorian.

The beginning of the American Studies major, Urban Studies major, etc. The Pass/Fail program.

The national victory in the GE College Bowl when another university complained because they thought Ed Leahey, FC '68, was a faculty member.

The discussions concerning the

University calendar and exams before Christmas.

The generosity of the pre-med and pre-law advisers.

The beginning of Alpha Mu Gamma, the foreign language honor society.

The emergence of new student publications.

The opening of Walsh Hall, a/k/a. 555—and problems with the neighbors.

The Arena registration where numerous problems were solved on the spot. The students' tactics in their effort to get into courses already closed.

The Gelhorn report and its consequences, real and imaginary.

The numerous victories of the Debate Society.

Intramurals finally removed from Edwards Parade Grounds.

The opening of Faculty Memorial Hall with many offices for student activities.

REV. HENRYK MISIAK

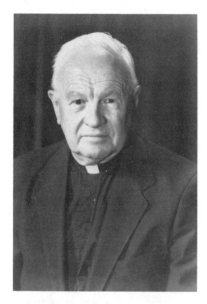

Rev. Henryk Misiak has been associated with Fordham since 1944, first as a doctoral student and then, from 1946, a a teacher in the Psychology Department. He has been Professor Emeritus since 1980. As a young priest, he fled Poland after the Nazi Invasion in 1939.

The Nazis began to deport, arrest, and even execute all the Poles whom they regarded as obstacles to the Germanization of the western part of Poland. Their prime target became the clergy. In the fall of 1939, most of my fellow priests as well as some of my family were arrested by the Gestapo and mostly deported to concentration camps like Dachau and Auschwitz. I knew the Gestapo was looking for me.

In December 1939, I succeeded in crossing the border to Slovakia, then to Hungary. From Hungary I went to France, and, after the creation of the Vichy government in that country, to Great Britain. It was there that I began my studies in experimental psychology. I received a modest fellowship to continue my studies in the United States. My original plan was to study at the Catholic University in Washington, D.C., but when I got there, I realized that my fellowship was inadequate. Thus, when the generous and kind Carmelite Sisters of St. Patrick's Home in the Bronx offered me lodging there, I came to New York and enrolled at Fordham in the Ph.D. program in psychology. The Department soon offered me a graduate assistantship which made things easier for me.

My speciality became neuropsychology. I took post-doctoral courses at Columbia University, in neuroanatomy, endocrinology, and sensory physiology. I was also associated with the neurology departments of St. Vincent's Hospital and Bellevue Hospital. Therefore I taught physiological psychology for 34 years at both undergraduate and graduate levels. Since this course was required of all psychology students, I had the opportunity to know all the students of the department. Of course, I taught several other courses, such as Structure and Function of the Brain, Psychopharmacology, and History of Psychology.

The Department initially was very strongly oriented toward experimental psychology, and the emphasis was on solid laboratory training. That is why, when we moved to Dealy Hall, we built a large animal laboratory with an operating room. Clinical orientation prevailed, and the program of clinical psychology became the largest program in the Department in the early 1960s. Two other programs were created: psychometrics, around 1960, and developmental psychology in 1971.

A few events which, in my opinion, were the most significant for the Department during my association with it included: Fordham hosting the annual convention of the Eastern Psychological Association in 1946; Anne Anastasi joining the faculty of the Department in 1947 and teaching until 1979; a grant of $250,000 from the federal government and a matching fund from the University to expand our facilities and move from Keating Hall to larger quarters in the renovated Dealy Hall, in 1965; the decision by the Department to accept only Ph.D. candidates to the graduate program; and creation of the clinical psychology program in 1958, its accreditation by the American Psychological Association, and the successful direction of this program by Dr. Marvin Reznikoff from 1968 to 1981.

Up to the retirement of Father Joseph Keegan there were always Jesuits on the Department's faculty. There are none now. At one time there were four, including Father William Bier, who was chairman of our Department for ten years, from 1958 to 1968, when he became Associate Academic Vice President of Fordham.

Several years after World War II I was asked to join the Polish section of the Voice of America and to give weekly religious radio talks in Polish. These talks would be transmitted to Munich, Germany and then broadcast over The Voice of America to Poland. I agreed and did this work for 33 years. For the last 20 years, they were entitled "Spiritual Values in America." I discussed various religious events in the United States, religious publications and views and discussions on current moral and spiritual problems. Of course, I taped my talks, sometimes two months in advance.

REV. JOSEPH F. MITROS, S.J.

Rev. Joseph F. Mitros, S.J., has been Professor Emeritus in the Theology Department since his retirement in 1982. He earned his doctorate in philosophy from Fordham in 1955.

I enrolled in the Department of Philosophy intending to get acquainted with the currents of American thought and the way of life in the United States, the place of my future work. The philosophy of religion of Edgar Sheffield Brightman became the topic of my dissertation. Personalistic idealism came to be the center of my orientation. History of ancient philosophy, a background for the history of Christianity, the transcendental philosophy of Immanuel Kant, the shaper of European thought of the future, and Augustine, the source of inspiration, for better or worse, of the Chris-

tian world views to come, turned out to be the subjects of my study.

Jesuit Fathers and lay people constituted the faculty. The most prominent among them, a man of international renown, was Dr. von Hildebrand, a refugee from Nazism, an inspiring and enthusiastic educator, a deeply religious man albeit in his own way.

In my teaching career, I was engaged at first in the Department of Languages (German) and then in the Department of Theology. I taught undergraduate theology in Fordham College and in the Graduate School of Religious Education. The subjects and the method of teaching were rather traditional. This fact somewhat puzzled me.

I made my theological undergraduate, and then doctoral, studies at the Gregorian University and Biblical Institute in Rome. There was a mixture of tradition and progress in the field of Biblical and extra-Biblical fields, particularly after the encyclical *Divino Afflante Spiritu* (1943), the Magna Carta for Scriptural studies in the Catholic Church. Hellenism and the Christian World (Prümm), the ancient Persian religion (Messina), Hinduism, the Old Testament (Bea), the classical and ancient Christian world (Patristics) at the secular University of Rome opened my intellectual horizons.

In America, meanwhile, new winds started blowing in the

Catholic Church, bringing the fresh air of revival. A scholarly approach to Scriptural studies with their form and redaction criticism, an unadulterated study of the history of Christianity, and ecumenism leaped rapidly into motion and spread widely to every institution. All that, not only in America, but also in Europe, led to the liberating explosion of theology before and after the Second Vatican Council.

The intellectual and spiritual upheaval in the Church at large was reflected in the Department of Religion as well as in the whole University. The Department of Theology, in addition to undergraduate courses in Scripture and comparative religion, as well as the history of Christianity, opened, under Father Gleason, graduate studies to offer the M.A. and Ph.D. in theology. Courses were offered and seminars directed in systematic theology, in the Old and New Testament; in history of Christianity: Patristics, Middle Ages, modern times, American Church history; in moral theology, ethics, Protestant history, history of the liturgy; history of Eastern religions: India, China, Japan, Islam; and the religions of American Indians.

Professional experts were hired: Catholic and Protestant. As far as the administration of the Department was concerned, it underwent a long and painful period of development by trial and error, by conflict and compromise. At first, the business was run rather autocratically by chairmen. Later on, the faculty became more and more involved; a division of theology into sections (systematic, Scriptural, historical, etc.) helped in handling problems more expeditiously. There was even a time when an executive committee of three did, less successfully, the work. In connection with this method of running the Department, a joke was coined: "Do you know the difference between the Russian 'troika' and the theology 'troika?' " Response: "The Russian 'troika' has a horse sense."

I taught during this period in the College: History of Oriental Religions and History of Patristic and Medieval Theology; in the Graduate School: Patristics, the Development of Papacy in the Ancient Church, and Historical Methodology.

STELLA E. MOUNDAS

Stella E. Moundas began her nearly 40 years of service at Fordham as a secretary in the office of the Dean of Fordham College, where she remained for 14 years. During that time she worked with Deans Charles Loughran, Leo McLaughlin, Lincoln Walsh, and George McMahon, all of whom she recalls with great affection. She then served Fordham as Secretary to three University Presidents, Fathers Leo McLaughlin, Michael Walsh, and James Finlay. Since 1987, she has been the Coordinator of Fordham's Sesquicentennial Celebration, including the Sesquicentennial Oral History Project.

The Assistant Dean of Fordham College, Father Charles Loughran, hired me as a clerk, especially to type envelopes for a few months. I must have eventually done something right, since I was asked to come back in September by both the Chairman of the Physics Department, Dr. Lynch, and Father Leo McLaughlin, who was then Dean. I chose the Dean's Office even though I would be earning $5 less per week there than in the Physics Department.

Working for Father Mc-Laughlin was certainly a memorable experience. He was a very dynamic Dean who was extremely popular with the students. In addition to his responsibilities as Dean, he taught English and oversaw senior retreats. He was clearly gifted as an instructor. He felt it essential that a teacher love his students.

My career in the President's Office began just after Father McLaughlin had been installed. I had the distinction of being the first woman to be hired as secretary to the President.

Father Michael Walsh was the next President under whom I served. I recall Father Walsh as always being a very hard worker. In fact, he usually gave me 12 to 15 tapes of dictation at a time after he had spent a weekend, as he put it, "reflecting"! Father Walsh was something of a paradox. He always wanted me to schedule a full day's appointments, but I always knew when he was tired because he would call out to me, "Darling, are you trying to kill me with so many appointments?"

I always was so sad when there

was a change of administration. Just before Father Walsh left the office on his last day, after saying goodbye to the others, I was the last. We hugged and both of us cried. Just then, someone knocked on the door, and when I opened it Father Finlay was there. He looked with amazement at the sight of two sniffling administrators.

Of all the Presidents for whom I've worked, I found Father Finlay the most enjoyable because he had such an even disposition. I found him warm and friendly. For example, he just loved Christmas. Every Christmas there was a wonderful party for the staff, alive with holiday spirit.

One of my major annual projects involved organizing the Christmas Concert. The University has always sought to celebrate this holiday as a community and as a family. I viewed my role as assisting in the creation of an atmosphere that made the event joyous for students, faculty, alumni, community people, and parents. A feeling of warmth. I might add that, being a Greek Orthodox, I enjoyed real educational experiences at Fordham,

from learning about the Catholic celebration of Christmas to the Jesuit view of spiritual life.

I had the unforgettable privilege of coordinating the inauguration of Father O'Hare to the Presidency of the University. It turned out to be a great success, and I was very proud of Fordham and Father O'Hare that day. In fact, the inauguration made the front page of *The New York Times* the next day.

Among the greatest joys of my years at Fordham are the many relationships I have established. It has been tremendous experiencing the humanity and warmth of world-class scholars who, at a personal level, in socializing with me, revealed an intellectual, spiritual, and human side of which others might not have been aware.

I am delighted that Father O'Hare assigned me as Coordinator of the Sesquicentennial. In this capacity, particularly with respect to the Oral History Project, I am privileged to be at the center of the history-making Sesquicentennial. Moreover, this position enabled me to start and bring to completion a project of which I am very proud.

HONORABLE WILLIAM HUGHES MULLIGAN

A 1939 cum laude graduate of Fordham College and a 1942 cum laude graduate of Fordham University's School of Law, William Hughes Mulligan was Dean of the Law School from 1956 to 1971. He was then appointed to the United States Court of Appeals, Second Circuit. He left the bench in 1981 to become a partner in the law firm of Skadden, Arps, Slate, Meagher & Flom. Fordham University conferred on Judge Mulligan in 1975 the honorary degree of Doctor of Laws in recognition of his distinguished career.

I was brought up in The Bronx. I always insist on "The." The only other places I know of with the article are The Vatican and The Hague. In the Bronx in those days there was a heavy number of Irish and Italian families and also some Jewish families. But, no matter what your ethnic background, you were identified by your parish. You were from Tolentine, Our Lady of Mercy, or, if you were particularly fortunate, Our Lady of Refuge.

The normal course in those days was for a boy to go to Fordham Prep or Regis, if he were bright, or some local Catholic high school and then automatically apply to Fordham College. I went to Cathedral College because I thought I had a vocation and then applied to Fordham. I would say that the vast majority of the students at the College then were locals. I could walk to school. There were some outlanders from Brooklyn, but the vast majority were New Yorkers. The boarders were primarily football players and other athletes. There were very few facilities for residents. I think we had maybe one or two dorms and that was it. St. John's Hall was the prime one for seniors and Dealy Hall for freshmen.

Ignatius Wiley Cox was probably, I think, the best Jesuit professor I ever had. He was idolized by my class, the class of '39, which produced some great Jesuits like Father Bill Hogan, Father John Donohue, Father Joe Dolan and several others—Bob Gleason, Bob Sealy. Cox was able to control a class of 300 people, which would be almost impossible today.

To do that he would ask a question and propose something and call on Mr. Boyle and say, "Mr. Boyle, is that clear to you?" and Boyle would say, "Yes." Then he'd say, "Mr. So and So, is that clear to you?" And then he would continue on until he had about seven fellows up and he would say to the last guy, "Is this as clear as a mountain lake in springtime?" And when the fellow said, "Yes," he would say "What is clear?" And that kept everybody on their toes. But, in any event, it was a great teaching technique, and years later when I was on the bench, I wrote several opinions in which I used the expression that this point of law was as clear as a mountain lake in springtime.

Mary Long was a girl from Halifax, Nova Scotia, who came to New York and whose first job was as a clerk in the Law School and she spent her whole life there. She was extremely rigid. She had her favorites and when I became Dean, somebody said, "Well, who's the Dean now?" She said, "Well, the Dean was Dean Wilkinson, then we had Mr. Finn, and now we have Billy Mulligan." She considered me a child.

She did everything by hand; all the grades and everything were entered by hand. She was also very frugal. For example, on the last day of examinations, Mary would come in with envelopes and pass them out to all us students and say, "Please write your name and address on there and we will mail your marks. We're doing this because if there is any mistake in the address, it's your own fault and not ours." Of course, the real reason was to save money. To have a girl come in to type up this stuff was something she couldn't stand. She would not send out the class schedules to the faculty until the first faculty meeting. She said. "Then you can pass them out." This was when a stamp was, you know, three cents. But that's the way she had been taught by Dean Wilkinson. The Law School was run on a shoestring.

In 1952, when Dean Wilkinson died and the University selected George Bacon as Acting Dean, George at that point was in his early 60s and was considered too old for the Deanship. George also said to Father McGinley, "I don't believe that a Protestant should become Dean of a Catholic Law School." You see how long ago this was. George was Acting Dean for two years. In 1954 John Finn was appointed Dean, and I was named Assistant Dean. Father Quain told me years later that I was the first choice of the committee, but I was too young. I was only thirty-six years old, so they didn't feel that the Law School could be entrusted to an infant.

On the other hand, John Finn was highly recognized, had high visibility in the community, and it was decided that the compromise would be to make Finn the Dean and me the Assistant Dean.

I was asked to keep an eye on Finn, who at this point had established that he was more interested in practicing law than in deaning. The first year he was Dean, he argued some 17 appeals in the New York Court of Appeals and the Second Circuit. He was doing too many things, and this upset some of the faculty and alumni. So, in 1956, Father McGinley called me during the summer and told me that I was to be the Dean.

The greatest thing in my life, outside of my family, has been my association with Fordham as a student, teacher, Dean, and trustee.

ANDREW B. MYERS

Dr. Andrew B. Myers began his Fordham teaching career in 1946 as an Instructor of English in Fordham College. After 24 years as an Assistant and Associate Professor, he rose to the rank of Professor in 1975 and served until 1986 when he became Professor Emeritus. His many Rose Hill appointments included Chairman of the English Department, President of the Faculty Senate, and Chairman of the University Library Committee and the University Research Council.

I graduated from Fordham in the Class of 1940, having come here as a sophomore in the summer of 1937 as a transfer student from St. Peter's. I was a callow sixteen. But I had known Fordham many years before that. My mother used to take me occasionally to Bronx Park, from our home in Elmhurst in Queens, in the middle of the 1920s. I was then quite young, born in 1920.

We came up on the Third Avenue El, in the clanking trains that aren't there any longer, and came downstairs and took a trolley car along Fordham Road, past the College grounds to the Bronx Zoo. But she always stopped, at one point, either coming or going, and walked me on campus to see if there was anybody there she knew. She had been a nurse on Wards Island, and the chaplains there, particularly in the summertime, were always Jesuits from Fordham.

There were some very formidable figures in my Fordham experience. Among the English teachers, Gabe Liegey was a no-nonsense, striking disciplinarian in the classroom, a brilliant teacher, and the father of 14 children, which fazed us. I think one of the high moments of my very early life as a young instructor was to be introduced to Mrs. Liegey, who was herself something of a legend. Also, Sam Telfair, who like Gabe Liegey is now departed, was a Southern gentleman to the nth degree, and another no-nonsense teacher we hugely admired. Then there was loyal Pat Kenneally, one of the many immigrant assistants on the campus in those days. Curmudgeon Pat was famous for his work in the Athletic Department, like helping the budget by cutting soap in half for sweaty athletes to lather with, whether they liked it or not.

There was a strong sense of family on campus. By and large we all knew—since many of us were from Jesuit high schools to begin with—what was expected of us, and followed through. I don't think we quite understood how rigorous the intellectual training actually was because we'd been living with it for years. You found out later, particularly in the war years, when we scattered all over the world and rubbed shoulders with people from other schools, just how first-class our education was.

In the immediate postwar years, when the student body exploded in numbers, there wasn't enough room for faculty offices of one kind or another. So Fordham dragooned somebody to give us wooden Navy barracks, two stories high, with wooden exits and entrances, that had been declared unfit for human habitation by the military. They were placed behind the gymnasium where there then was a lot of grass and open space and given names like Reidy Hall and King-O'Neill—the names of war casualties. They were an experience. The stairs creaked, the floors shook under you. You kept waiting for the moment in which you had to leap out a window in case they burnt down.

It was a very different atmosphere on campus many years later during the Vietnam War, especially when some misguided students occupied the Administration building. I was the President of the Faculty Senate at the time, and my office was in that building. My secretary was a grand older lady, a feisty gal, Mrs. Rose Pierce, who came from the Italian-American colony across Fordham Road. She took no nonsense from anybody, including whoever happened to be signing the letters she typed.

I was in class one morning, early, when I heard a kind of uproar outside. I continued teaching until the end of the hour, at which point I discovered that when Rose got in that morning, she opened her desk drawer and found what looked exactly like a bomb. A cruel trick, unworthy of Fordham. You might have expected her to faint or run to the far end of the building and get out screaming. Not Rose. She resolutely picked up the bomb— the police later determined it was a fake—and stomped out of the building with people dodging her in all directions, she muttering words no one knew the lady knew beforehand, and flung the contraption on the lawn to blow up if it chose.

I have always found that librarians are the unsung heroes and heroines of our profession. They do almost everything they do, particularly at Duane Library, with grace and in a most unselfish fashion. I pay tribute to all those I have known over the years, especially directors like Joe Hart and later Anne Murphy. A library, in many ways, is the heart of studies at Fordham, outside of the classroom. It's a wonder house of books and staff people.

On reflection, I got older, I got sadder, and I don't think I got any wiser, but one thing I have taken with me from Fordham that has always enriched my life, is that I met my beloved wife, Margaret, "Maggie," here at Fordham. In 1946, my first year of teaching, I noticed that one biology graduate student in Larkin Hall, who had a cubicle near the upstairs science classroom, was getting altogether too much attention from one of my freshman, veteran students who liked a bit too much to corral her after class and pester her for a date.

He turned out to be a very nice guy, but I had to blow the whistle on him and tell him to leave the girl alone. Well, he took this from his teacher, but the girl stared at me with much relief and then fled back to her cubicle. To make a long story short, we wound up holding hands in the Rose Hill moonlight and getting married. After nearly 40 years we are still very much together. *Deo gratias!*

JOHN NELSON

Dr. John Nelson was a co-founder of and professor in Fordham's Graduate School of Religion and Religious Education beginning in 1964. He also taught theology at Fordham Prep from 1962 to 1970. He earned his doctorate in theology at Fordham in 1972.

The Graduate School of Religion and Religious Education

Partly because of our smaller numbers (we make up slightly more than one per cent of the University), our School has a closeness and intensity all its own. Thus my experience of Fordham may be quite different from that of professors in other Schools and Departments—although I think that they too are most at home in their own smaller neighborhoods.

In my quarter of a century at Fordham the University has had special crises in trying to own and express its academic identity. For example, are we a teaching university or a research university? We would like to achieve excellence in both but often do not quite reach it in either—although we keep trying. Are we integrated into the life of New York City and of the Bronx? Or are we oases of separation and isolation for the sake of study and reflection? Again, we do a bit of both and don't always succeed at either.

Both professionally and personally, I have felt myself part of these crises.

I did my doctoral work in theology in the late 1960s. In those years just after the Second Vatican Council, theology in a university rather than a seminary setting was booming. Fordham shared in the boom with excellent faculty members and outstanding graduate students. The Department was pulled in at least two directions. One direction was to offer something of everything: Eastern religions, Biblical languages, Protestant religious traditions, etc. The other direction was to concentrate upon what was more particular to the Catholic theological tradition. I favored the latter direction, especially in a city with other outstanding schools of theology. I greatly respect our Theology Department, but I do wish it had moved more decisively then toward depth in the Catholic tradition.

Two brief histories of the Graduate School of Religion and Religious Education are available. One, authored by our current Dean and one of our School's founders, Father Vincent Novak, S.J., traces its structural development and is contained in the School's five-year plan. The second, entitled "Some Historical Notes on Curriculum in Fordham's GSRRE," which I wrote, deals with curricular development.

Our School began in the mid-1960s in response to a need: people wanted to learn Scripture, theology, and human sciences in a way that could make them teachers and pastoral workers in the spirit of the Second Vatican Council. Students came in large numbers. In summers we had class sizes as high as one hundred; we ran institutes with one thousand or more registrants. Students came of high quality: from those early years we have many alumni who have been writers, teachers, and administrators in important positions over the years.

In the 1970s there was a leveling-off of numbers, but a continued strength. The "Fordham experience" in the Graduate School of Religion and Religious Education was a good one for our students. I recall especially the steady stream of students from countries like Australia who returned to positions of responsibility in their native lands.

More recent memories, those in the 1980s, are of innovation in course offerings while at the same time maintaining a tradition of academic substance. The fact that we have maintained ourselves in a market smaller in numbers and competitive in programs reflects a certain success in what we have been trying to accomplish.

Some of my strongest memories are of friendships with both faculty members and students. For the last few years, for example, our Scripture professor Peter Ellis, who has just recently retired, stayed over with us once a week. Those were very pleasant evenings with someone who shared ideas and ideals.

Get-togethers with students have been part of our history. Our students usually range in age from about twenty-five to fifty-five. Most come to Fordham with several years of pastoral or educational experience. They are eager to listen and eager to share, but in an adult kind of way. This makes it very satisfying and enriching to spend time with them.

In our School we have a tradition also of prayer and worship. Three times a year, for example, our students organize a liturgy and social in honor of those who are finishing their requirements for their degree. From time to time a friend or family member of one of our students may become seriously ill or die. To offer sympathy and support we join together in celebrating the Eucharist. We have been a School that is more than a school.

REV. EUGENE J. O'BRIEN, s.j.

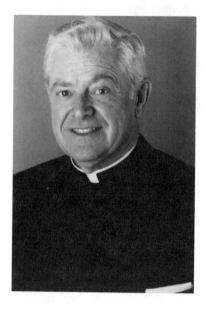

Rev. Eugene J. O'Brien, s.j., began his Fordham career as an instructor at Fordham Prep from 1950 to 1953. He served as Headmaster of the Prep from 1960 to 1970, as Headmaster–President from 1970 to 1975, and as President from 1975 to 1979. He led the effort for a new Prep building at Rose Hill and oversaw the separate incorporation of the Prep from the University. On January 13, 1980, the University awarded him the Insignis Medal, an honor previously accorded to such distinguished recipients as Francis Cardinal Spellman, Vincent T. Lombardi, and Rev. Harold Mulqueen, s.j. Father O'Brien returned to Fordham University in 1986 as Assistant to the President. In 1987 he was appointed Vice President for University Relations.

I knew it was an important day when the then President of the University, Father Michael Walsh, phoned in the fall of 1968 to ask if he could come over to see me at the Prep. He wanted to discuss the legal separation of the Prep from the University. By this time, the Jesuit Community and the University had already been separately incorporated, and Fordham was governed by a lay-majority Board of Trustees. The reason for that change and the thinking behind the suggestion that the Prep also be separately incorporated were the same—the University's anticipated application for state financial aid under the Bundy Law. Mr. Walter Gelhorn, a member of the faculty of Columbia University Law School, who was advising Fordham on the issue of state aid, recommended the moves.

At our meeting, I told Father Walsh that I welcomed the proposal because I felt it was the right move at that time, not only for the University and its financial considerations, but also for the Prep itself. If the Prep was to undertake a major capital campaign for a new building and to secure its long-term financial well-being, it needed its own board of trustees, people who joined its board primarily because they were interested in secondary education. So Father Walsh and I had a very easy meeting of minds, especially because he was one of the most wonderful people in the world to work with.

Father Walsh had consulted

with the Jesuit Provincial of the New York Province before asking me. Subsequently it became clear that Jesuit headquarters in Rome had some concerns since we were effectively creating a new form of governance for our high schools. In July of 1970, while visiting Rome and at the suggestion of our New York Provincial, I took the opportunity to talk with the Superior General of the Order, Father Pedro Arrupe.

I wanted to clear up any misconceptions of how we had reached the decision to incorporate Fordham Prep separately and what it would mean for the School's future. At that time, Rome was still not sure of the change that a good number of the Jesuit universities, including Fordham, had made in moving from a purely religious board of trustees to a board composed of both lay and religious. I assured the General that I saw the arrangement we had made as the only solution for American Jesuit high schools. In one of the more remarkable sentences I have ever heard, Father General said to me, "I have learned much today."

Within six months, he wrote a letter to the entire American Assistancy (the Jesuits in the United States), in which he explained some guidelines he wished to see in the future development of Jesuit secondary schools in the United States. One of those guidelines emphasized our "colleagueship" with lay men and women, not only as teachers, but as administrators and policy makers for our schools. That was a landmark document, and I've always had the feeling that maybe the talk we had that day at least facilitated, or possibly expedited, his writing it. We are talking about a piece of history that is today so commonly accepted and understood that all our schools now find themselves with boards of trustees, and they have been their salvation.

For assistance in all of this, on the advice of the Chancellor of the New York State Board of Regents, Mr. Joseph W. McGovern (a graduate of Regis High School, Fordham College, and Fordham Law School), I consulted with Lawrence X. Cusack (also Regis High School, Fordham College, and Fordham Law), senior partner of the firm Cusack and Stiles. His enormous understanding of church–state relationships in American law was immensely helpful to us as we selected a model for the governance of Fordham Prep. He happened also to be a very valued and constantly called-upon legal counsel to Cardinal Spellman and his successor, Terence Cardinal Cooke.

Mr. Cusack suggested a double-tier board in which the owners of the Fordham Prep Corporation would be a group of seven Jesuits, including the executive officer of the Prep and a representative of the Provincial, to be called The Board of Members. They in turn would elect the Board of Trustees, and the trustees would set the policy for governing the School and elect its executive officer, as well as work with the Prep's administration on a regular basis.

The reaction of the Prep alumni to all this was very positive once it was explained. Indeed any problems disappeared once they understood that the move would help the University develop its financial resources, that the Prep was remaining on the campus, that the University had deeded a piece of its property to us, and that we would continue to use some of the University's facilities, such as the Church, Collins Auditorium, and some playing fields. The separate incorporation of the Prep from the University took place in June 1970.

We did succeed in constructing a marvelous new building for the Prep, which opened in September 1972. The cost of the new facility and the need to endow the School, especially in order to provide financial aid to needy students, necessitated a great deal of fund raising. In the spring of 1976, the Board of Trustees decided we needed a major fund-raising event and instructed me to think of one. After a long weekend with my Development Director, John J. Cummings, I came up with nothing, until I opened the Arts and Leisure section of the Sunday *New York Times*. There I read an interview with Bing Crosby, who was asked why he was still doing benefit concerts at the age of 75. He replied, "There are a lot of nice songs to sing, and lots of nice causes to help."

The next day, I called out to Bellarmine Prep in San Jose, a Jesuit school, where Mr. Crosby's son Harry was then a student. I asked the president for the telephone number of the Crosby home. His initial response was less than trusting, but he agreed to make the call and see if Mr. Crosby would speak with me. He asked me not to ask Bing Crosby for a gift, and I did not. Instead, I asked him to consider doing a concert for us, and the answer was yes. It was that simple.

The concert took place the following December. He had not sung in New York in 45 years. We used Avery Fisher Hall at Lincoln Center and we filled the house, making almost $200,000 for the Prep. Mr. Crosby died in October of 1977. We later had a second benefit performance by Mr. Crosby's good friend Bob Hope.

The Crosby concert had a tremendous psychological impact on our efforts to retire a debt of nearly $3 million. The attention given the concert in the newspapers and on television seemed to convince people that if we could stage such a successful event, we could also solve our financial problems. It was right after that that we started the "Burn the Mortgage" campaign. Indeed, under the leadership of Governor

Malcolm Wilson, a triple Fordham graduate, we burned the mortgage and cleared the Prep of all debt by December 1979.

JOHN C. OLIN

Dr. John C. Olin began his 40-year tenure in the Fordham College History Department as an instructor in 1946. He was appointed a full Professor in 1970 and became Professor Emeritus in 1986.

One of the big differences was the absence of autos and the lack of the need for security on the campus. When I first came here we had one campus cop and his main job, I think, was to keep some of the neighborhood kids off the grass. A more important difference perhaps is the change that occurred in the Jesuit presence and in the type of curriculum. Scholastic philosophy, of course, was one of the mainstays in the 1930s, along with the Classics, along with Latin and Greek.

All that has disappeared, save for the Classics Department, of course; that is one of many now. And that old *Ratio Studiorum*, as we called it, has long since been buried. Prayers before class, crucifixes in the classroom, and the devotions that took place every day in May are gone too. I don't mean to say that such a thing as religious commitment has vanished entirely, but it manifests itself in an entirely different way now.

I came to Fordham to get a master's degree in history a few years after graduating from Canisius College in Buffalo. The professor I had then that impressed me the most was Ross Hoffman. I did my master's thesis with him in 1941. I got to know Ross quite well after I returned from my naval service in the War. He was an impressive professor to say the least. I thought I would love to be a teacher like him. He was so dramatic and well ordered in class, and I was very much impressed with his method of teaching as well as his content. He did inspire me.

I began by teaching medieval history, which was the required history course that students took in their sophomore year. For some reason, as I began to teach additional things, I became interested in the Renaissance and the Reformation. Perhaps there was a gap in the Department that I filled. I became particularly interested in the person of Erasmus and his thought. Actually, Erasmus was an interest of mine way back when I was at Canisius. I had heard about him in a history course, and he seemed to be a very attractive figure, and I liked his ideas. After I completed my dissertation, I began to teach in the Graduate School.

I have been involved with organizing conferences at Fordham on Thomas More and the Reformation. The first conference, in 1967, which was jointly sponsored with Union Theological Seminary, was on the 450th anniversary of Martin Luther's Ninety-five Theses. By that time Vatican II had taken place and ecumenism was in the air, and everybody was leaning over backward to agree with the other side, or to try to understand the other side. The next conference, in 1977, commemorated the 500th anniversary of the birth of Thomas More.

When I first came to Fordham I was considered the liberal in the History Department, both politically and religiously. I don't exactly like the word liberal anymore, or conservative either, because I think those are cliché labels that aren't too meaningful anymore. But I was anti-McCarthy, for example, probably one of the few in this ambience that was, and I was very outspoken about it. When I spoke in class sometimes about McCarthy and what he was doing, it was so much to the dissatisfaction of the class that on one occasion I remember everyone in the class got

up and turned their chairs around and I talked to their backs.

I was also an ardent supporter of Adlai Stevenson. I was a real "egghead," as he was called, and then I guess I was religiously liberal. I was certainly solidly Catholic and orthodox but perhaps I took more liberal views than most. Now the world has moved far to my left and, although I feel I have more or less retained my same outlook and views, I've become more conservative in my general attitudes.

In the late 1970s there was great talk on campus about "values education," which I took vigorous exception to. The idea of having a certain segment of the curriculum or courses specifically devoted to values seemed to me totally ridiculous. Even more than that, all education, I thought, is a matter of values and you can't separate values as some specific topic that can be discussed one or two days a week in class.

I think my stance offended Father Bob Roth, who was the Dean of Fordham College and the man behind the program. I suppose his ideas and purpose were very good, the need to stress values which are so frequently neglected in secular education. But the way to do that is to stress education itself as a matter of discussing and dealing with values. The educated man is a man with values. Besides, I think many of the so-called curriculum revisions do not make an awful lot of difference—as long as you have some good teachers making the students think and work (that's the important thing) and relating them to their heritage as civilized human beings.

GILDA PETRAGLIA

Dr. Gilda Petraglia retired in 1986 after more than 33 years as a professor in the School of Social Work, which later became the Graduate School of Social Service. She earned her doctorate from Fordham in 1965.

When I first came to Fordham, the School of Social Service was on 39th Street and Lexington Avenue, and it consisted of a double brownstone building; there were three classrooms in the building, a chapel, and a room that contained a library. So they were rather tight quarters but, at that point, we had primarily a two-year program in social work. We did not have the range of programs that have developed over the course of 33 years.

When we moved to Lincoln Center, it was really an exciting experience in a number of ways.

One, we were going to have increased facilities, and that was very important because we wanted to grow. Secondly, it meant that the School of Social Work, the School of Education, and the School of Law were now going to be in close proximity to one another. It was the hope, not only of the University, but also of the faculty, that being closer together we would develop ties that would increase the University's goal for excellence.

Although I am not Pollyanish enough to think that it was achieved once we got together, we did develop better relationships, so that we did have an opportunity to use each other's resources, to influence each other's thinking.

One good example was the Summer Head Start Programs that were held in the late 1960s. The Archdiocese of New York had contracted with the School of Social Service to train some of their staff, and then we included some of the people from the School of Education to help us develop the program for two summers. It was really a fascinating way of working. The Law School got into the picture by providing the facilities because at that point their facilities were completed, while we were waiting for the building to be developed for the School of Education and the School of Social Service.

One of the people who were very important in getting these

programs developed was Jim Dumpson, who stands out as one of the very concerned Deans of the School of Social Service; he helped us in seeing the necessity of moving not only within the University, but out into the community. Dean Mary Ann Quaranta, who is the current dean, has continued what Jim Dumpson started. Another dean who stands out in my mind is Anna King, who really encouraged faculty to move ahead on projects, on ideas, and to facilitate not only the School's participation, but the community's as well. And Dean Mottola at the School of Education was very effective in helping us to work together and to develop our ideas and thinking.

I was very disappointed when the Social Work program was discontinued in the undergraduate school in 1984. We had been able to attract quite a number of students who were effective in delivering services to the poor, to the needy, students who were not going to go on for their master's degree, but who were going into rather productive positions in social work which did not require the master's degree. Unfortunately, the undergraduate faculty felt that the program was too much of a professional program for the Liberal Arts College. They felt that they should emphasize the liberal arts base and that the professional addition should come at the master's level.

In the 1960s, the School of So-

cial Service also saw a great need to emphasize curriculum content on institutional racism, not only to try and become effective in eradicating it, but to produce students who would be thinking of the need to eradicate it. As a faculty, we thought it should not be taught solely by one ethnic group, that the best way to teach this content would be to bring a diverse faculty together.

So we got volunteers among the Caucasian, black, and Hispanic faculty who were really interested in the topic. The University, through Dean Dumpson, was able to provide us with a modest stipend to invite guest speakers to share with us the latest thinking on how we could most effectively deliver a course on institutional racism. It was a tough struggle, and as much as we were motivated to do it, feelings ran high. We weren't always the most agreeable group, but eventually we were successful, and to this day there is a required course in institutional racism at the School.

Fordham changed me in that each year I realized how little I knew. When I first came to Fordham, I thought I knew a lot, and even when I got up to give a lecture, I could go rather rapidly in sharing what I knew and what I thought would be helpful to other people. Through the years, I've learned more and more about all the exceptions to the ideas I've developed, and I have come to the conclusion how much more I need to know in order to share effectively with other people. In other words, I felt I was smarter when I first came to Fordham!

CAESAR L. PITASSY

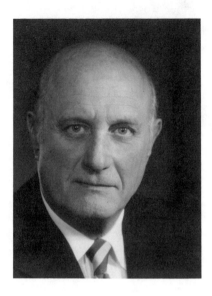

Photo by Bachrach

Caesar L. Pitassy is a 1941 graduate of Fordham Law School who served as editor-in-chief of the Law Review. *He later served as President of the Law School Alumni Association from 1959 to 1964. He was the managing partner of the law firm of Rogers & Wells.*

What led me to become a lawyer was a friend of mine. After I graduated from college in 1937, I went to work for my father, and a friend of mine by the name of Daniel Amend, of the Amend family of Fordham fame (at least two of his older brothers had gone to Fordham Law School), was working that year too. We were very friendly and used to do things together; one day during the summer we started talking about what we wanted to do and

he said, "You know, my brothers want me to go to law school. Why don't you come along with me?" So I said, "Okay."

It was that casual. And we applied to Fordham Law School and had no trouble getting in as long as we had the tuition. That was in 1938. Tuition was $200. There were three sessions, morning, afternoon, and night, and we went in the morning. The Law School was located in the Woolworth Building at 233 Broadway, and we went to school starting at 9 o'clock in the morning, finishing by 12 or 12:30.

At the *Law Review*, Professor Walter B. Kennedy was Moderator, and Professor William White was his assistant. They were mainly concerned with getting lead articles for the *Law Review*. We talked about other subjects to be covered in the *Law Review* and asked students to write notes. We picked cases out that students did case notes on. Whether a lead article was printed in the *Law Review* or not was up to Professor Kennedy.

We used to go down to the *Law Review* office after class. We'd have a little lunch and go to the office, and depending on the time of the year or whether the issue was coming out, we'd work well into the evening. At issue time when we had to make a printing or other deadline we might work all night.

We had some young professors who were excellent, including Joe

McGovern, Paul Carroll, and Frank Conway. Even after they left on a full-time basis of teaching, they stayed on as part-time professors.

Professor Wormser was deaf, but he could read your lips. He had a machine that he put on the desk that was supposed to help him hear, but the wires were never connected. You'd see the wires hanging out. But if that fooled you, you would be picked up in a hurry. And when you recited a case, he looked at you, and I'm sure he read your lips because he couldn't hear a word you said. He was an excellent professor.

We had a couple of professors who ran the moot court. George Bacon was one of them. We were split into teams and given cases to try. We prepared the case, argued the case, tried the case before a jury. We were assisted by the professors who helped us prepare our case. We didn't have the intermural moot court competition they have today. It was purely in the School. You weren't competing with anybody except people on the other side of your case.

My term as President of the Fordham Law Alumni Association was from 1959 to 1964. The President before me was Edward Schulkind, who ran it on sort of a part-time basis. The main function of the Law Alumni Association in those days was to have an annual luncheon to which they

would invite speakers. As a matter of fact, President John F. Kennedy was a speaker during the time he was a U. S. Senator. The dues, I remember, were practically nothing—maybe $10.

We expanded the activities of the Alumni Association. We tried to drum up the interest of the alumni. We published a directory, created a scholarship fund and other things, and got to be quite active. We continued with the annual luncheon. I think Schulkind had started monthly luncheons. We continued with those, and the Alumni Association grew. Dues were raised; contributions to the scholarship fund increased.

It was during my term that we created the position of the Executive Secretary. Frances Blake started in my regime. That helped a lot. She was the daughter of John Blake, a former professor.

I was given the Fordham Law Alumni Medal at the annual luncheon in 1972. William Hughes Mulligan presented it. It was a great day for me. As President, I had presented the medal to quite a few others. It was held where it's always held, in the main ballroom of the Waldorf Astoria.

Fordham Law School is truly a family tradition for me. My son is a graduate of the Law School. My sister and her husband were graduates as are my daughter-in-law and two of my nephews.

REV. WILLIAM L. REILLY, s.j.

Rev. William L. Reilly, S.J., had three tours of service at Fordham, beginning as an instructor at Fordham Prep from 1940 to 1942. He moved to Fordham College to teach in the Philosophy Department from 1947 to 1954 and later served as Associate Academic Vice President from 1980 to 1985. From 1964 to 1975 he served as President of LeMoyne College in Syracuse.

Life was a lot simpler when I began at Fordham. For example, in the summer of 1939, my first at Rose Hill, we had one fire warden and, as far as I know, not a single security guard. Life was that simple. I could walk around at night in the dark of the lightly lit quadrangle and say my prayers without the slightest concern. It was a life focused on the academic along with a very personal relationship of professor to student.

The University was all embracing from Rose Hill. I knew very little about the other schools that were located downtown. At Rose Hill, the Prep was a full member of the community and the atmosphere was one of total involvement. I used to go out after school and kick footballs with the Prep students. According to the formalities of that time, we were always in cassocks and birettas. It's always been fulfilling over the years to see how those students developed.

When I came back in 1947 we were in the full wave of welcoming and adapting to the veterans. My first class was two-thirds veterans; they were a fine group to teach. The other third were, if I may use the term, kids, because they had gone through high school in three years. That was my introduction to higher education. The tempo of life on the campus had changed somewhat. There was a great struggle for space for living, studying, and working. And increasingly we focused more on becoming a boarder campus.

It was around this time that the whole civil rights issue began to take hold, including on the campus. I had organized the Campus Interracial Council, and we started the Interracial Sunday here in 1951. So I welcomed the civil rights movement and the stress on affirmative action.

I taught the first black student at Fordham Prep, at least in recent history, Denis Baron. Denis was, later, around 1947–1948, the first black teacher in the Department of Economics. So I saw good will and outreach. As we look back now, it could have been done differently, but hindsight is always so much more effective. When I came back in 1950, after an interlude of a year in Montreal, I began to work downtown with Father LaFarge in the Catholic Interracial Council on Vesey Street. And in the previous year, when I taught at the School of Education, the great Dan Sullivan had started the first Fordham Interracial Council.

Interracial Sunday took place on the first or second Sunday of Lent. We would have a special mass, special preacher, as we called them in those days, and our Father LaFarge was here with us. So we were taking steps then which were part of the development, and, as we look back, too

slow development, of involving the minority students.

I was here for the Centennial in 1941. I was at the Prep at the time, and with the insouciance of youth we used to chuckle about some of the formalities. But I was down at the Waldorf the night of the grand banquet early that fall. As always, Father Gannon gave a magnificent address. It marked a stage of self-awareness and self-assurance on the part of alumni. We had a series of events on campus. I remember an extended solemn high mass and we had a special yearbook, *The Centurian.* Father Raymond Schouten, God rest his soul, was the Moderator.

It was Father Gannon's desire to broaden the base of the student population here at Rose Hill, and he offered—I can still hear him—to the number one graduate of any Jesuit prep school in the country a scholarship to come to Fordham. A good number of the very effective men who graduated in the early '40s were the first fruits of that effort.

PAUL J. REISS

Dr. Paul J. Reiss, who received a master's degree from Fordham in 1953, served Fordham in several key positions from 1963 to 1985. A sociology professor, Dr. Reiss was Chairman of the Department of Sociology from 1964 to 1968. In 1969–1970 he served as Dean of the College at Lincoln Center, and from 1969 to 1975, he was the University's Academic Vice President. From 1975 to 1985, Dr. Reiss was Fordham's Executive Vice President. He is now the President of St. Michael's College in Vermont.

I recall very fondly the early days after we moved to the east wing of Dealy Hall. At that time three departments were located on the fifth floor: Sociology, Economics, and Political Science. The chairman in Political Science was Father Jim Finlay. The chairman

in Economics was Dr. Joe Cammarosano. I didn't know it at that time, in working with these very fine persons and excellent academicians, that we would have close associations in the years to come in the administration of Fordham.

Joe Cammarosano became the President of the Faculty Senate, and then Father Finlay was appointed Dean of the Graduate School of Arts and Sciences, and I became Dean of the College at Lincoln Center. Then Joe Cammarosano was appointed, now with Father Walsh, as Executive Vice President. I was asked by Father Walsh to serve as Academic Vice President and then, with Father Walsh's departure, Father Finlay moved from the Graduate School to the Office of the President.

One of the strengths, I have always felt, of the administration at Fordham, during that period of time and subsequently, was that the major administrative positions, positions of Dean and Academic Vice President and other vice presidents were basically filled by people who had experience as faculty members at Fordham and who had close ties with members of the faculty. It, perhaps, was a more faculty-based administration that would be found at most universities.

The year 1969–1970 was a very difficult year. I had just gone through the first semester of trying to put The College at Lincoln

Center together when the Academic Vice President, Arthur Brown, resigned. It was at that time that Father Walsh, in his very kind and congenial way, asked me to serve as Acting Academic Vice President (this was in August) and he said, "Now, of course, we really don't have an opportunity at this time to go out and get a Dean to replace you at Lincoln Center, and in any event this is an acting Academic Vice President position, so perhaps you can do both jobs for the time that it will be necessary to do so."

It probably would have been more manageable had it not been an exceptional year at Fordham and throughout the country, because that was, perhaps, the year of greatest upsets and turmoil. I remember, in the spring of 1970, the Kent State incident had occurred, there was a major fire on the campus at Rose Hill, and the question was raised as to whether final exams should be held or students sent home.

Faculty had all sorts of opinions on the matter, and I was conducting a meeting of the faculty on this question when the secretary from Father McMahon's office put a note on the lectern informing me that the students had occupied my office at Lincoln Center wanting to know why it is that in this time of crisis their dean was not around. That sort of typified my year. . . .

This was also the time when there were protests over R.O.T.C., the occupation of the

Administration Building, and I recall how difficult it was to deal with that. I remember meeting in the Council Room with Father Walsh, Joe Cammorasano, and several others, trying to decide what we should do about the occupation of the south wing of the Administration Building. There were no basic rules and regulations to cover such matters since no one had envisioned that such things might happen.

The New York Police were about in plain clothes and more police were available on buses just off the campus. We felt that in addition to talking with the students that we must, in fact, get them out one way or another, hopefully in a peaceful manner. We tried to do that by utilizing Fordham's own security people.

In hindsight, that was probably a mistake. The sight of a security officer wedging a bar between the door and frame between the hallway and the President's Office while students were pushing up against the other side and throwing water at the security people was a terrible, terrible kind of sight. One wondered what one was getting to in the whole nature of higher education.

Eventually the students did leave, and some were charged with trespass. It's interesting that even while these things were going on the basic process of education at Fordham in its various schools continued without major interruptions. There was very serious turmoil, but except for the question of the fires and final exams that year, it did not prevent a real university education from going on and that was, of course, encouraging.

HARRY N. RIVLIN

Photo by Bachrach

Dr. Harry N. Rivlin was Professor of Education and Dean of the School of Education from 1966 to 1973. He then served as an Adjunct Professor from 1973 to 1978 and was the John Mosler Professor in the School of Education from 1973 to 1977. Dr. Rivlin has been Dean Emeritus and Professor Emeritus since 1977.

Before I came to Fordham, The Graduate School of Education was getting along fairly well. It was, however, not, quite The *Graduate* School of Education because at 302 Broadway The School of Education enrolled undergraduate students as well as graduate. It went all the way from the freshman year of a liberal arts college right through to the doctorate in The Graduate School of Education. When we moved to Lincoln Center, the separate College at Lincoln Center was established, and the School of Education became the Graduate School of Education.

Dr. Kathryn Scanlon Carlin, whom I knew through professional meetings, called me one day and said she'd like to come up to see me. Since I always met anybody who was willing to spend the bus fare or subway fare to come in, I had her come. After we made our polite inquiries about health and the weather, she told me that Fordham was looking for a new dean, and "we were wondering if you would come, but don't answer. Father Leo McLaughlin and Father Timothy Healy, they are interesting people, and you would enjoy meeting them."

So, I went up to see Father McLaughlin, who was the President, and Father Healy, the Executive Vice President. They told me that they had just about decided to close the School of Education because they thought it was a second-rate institution, and the Fordham they envisioned had no place for second-rate schools. But they didn't think it right for a Jesuit institution not to have a school of education.

It was my basic thesis in thinking about the School that if we could prepare teachers for one urban district, we could prepare them for all. I didn't know it, but that was exactly what Father McLaughlin and Father Healy had been thinking of. Their theme was that Fordham is an urban institution, so that my emphasis on preparing teachers for the urban schools fitted right into their plans. What began as a general discussion moved into the offer of a job.

While I was flattered, I was also taken aback. I wasn't coming for a job interview, and I pointed out that my coming to Fordham might not be a good idea. In the first place, I said, changing an institution around isn't a job for one year. It takes longer than a year. At the end of a year, they were going to be disappointed by the results or the lack of results. Second, I said, how would the faculty react to my coming in? I'm a stranger in every way you could define "stranger." I've had no contact with Fordham's School of Education. I am not a Jesuit. I am not even a Catholic. Wouldn't I be a complete outsider?

Father McLaughlin laughed his usual high cackle laugh and he said, "You were chosen by the faculty." He told me that the faculty, faced with extinction, presented a list of five names as the new Dean. My name was at the head of the list and crossed out. Father McLaughlin asked why the name was crossed out, and the answer was, "He won't come to Fordham." Then Father said, "I refuse to look at any list where the first name is crossed out and you didn't even ask him." We left it at that.

About a week later I got a letter from Father Healy. I don't remember the whole letter, but I'll give you the first sentence. He said, "In the best English tradition, we didn't discuss salary." He outlined, "if you see, well, if it is to your liking to come to Fordham," then he listed the things that Fordham would do. And to anticipate an expression that wasn't in use then, it was an offer you couldn't refuse.

I had always been in public education; this was my first contact with private education. I had always been with a non-sectarian school; this was my first affiliation with a church-related school, and it all worked out well, from my point of view. It's one of the most exciting professional experiences I've had in a professional life that was rather full of pleasant packages.

At my first meeting with the faculty, I remember saying that Fordham was in Manhattan, New York City, and the University of Kansas is in Manhattan, Kansas, and our catalogue ought not to look as though it were interchangeable with one in Manhattan, Kansas. What can we do to prepare our people for Manhattan, New York, knowing that if we did, they would also be welcome in Chicago and in St. Louis.

When I was through, there was polite applause, but no motion to commit it to a committee. Instead, somebody made the motion that "we endorse the plan in principle" (there really was no plan), and "we urge the dean to implement it at the earliest opportunity" and the meeting ended.

Later, Barbara Lake, a faculty member, asked me how I liked the first session and I said I liked it and she asked, "What are you going to do now?" I said, "Well, when we plan for September or for February we'll have to include planning time in the program for various people so we can put flesh on this outline." She asked, "How can you wait until February?" Then I remember saying, "Don't be silly. Who has the time to add this burden to their program when we can't change programs now." She made the classic answer, "How about me?"

So we started planning on the next day. I was a member of the American Association for Teacher Education Committee on Educating the Disenfranchised, the Disadvantaged. So I asked that committee to give us a little grant of about $18,000 and with that and the volunteer efforts of members of the faculty we were able to bring in anthropologists, economists, and people from various institutions.

By the end of the semester, we had a report giving a plan for the education of the disadvantaged of the urban community. On February 1 at 10 A.M., which was exactly five months and one hour after my official coming to Fordham, we had the first class meeting in the new program of urban education.

REV. ROBERT J. ROTH, s.j.

Rev. Robert J. Roth, s.j., earned his master's and doctoral degrees in philosophy from Fordham and has been a professor of philosophy in Fordham College since 1953. He was Dean of Fordham College from 1974 to 1979 and also served as President of the Faculty Senate from 1972 to 1974. From 1962 to 1967, Father Roth was the Jesuit Superior in Spellman Hall, the residence hall for Jesuit scholastics.

Spellman Hall formally opened in July 1947. It was originally planned and built as a residence hall for Jesuit priests and scholastics who were studying for graduate degrees at Fordham University and at other graduate schools in the New York City area, for example, Columbia, Yeshiva, and New York University. The building was named after Francis Car-dinal Spellman, then Archbishop of New York, who was an alumnus of Fordham College, Class of 1911, and who made a large contribution toward the completion of that building.

The plan was conceived by Rev. Robert I. Gannon, s.j., then President of Fordham University. He modeled it after the Jesuit residence at Cambridge University, England, where he himself had studied. Prior to 1947, Jesuits pursuing graduate degrees in New York City lived in various places on campus: the upper floors of Dealy Hall, the top floors of Hughes Hall, and the Administration Building.

In the summer of 1946 and 1947 I was a graduate student in philosophy. You can imagine the long climb we Jesuits had to make back and forth between classroom and the top floors of Dealy or Hughes. It did nothing for our brains, but it certainly strengthened our legs!

Spellman Hall filled a great need in its day and for this Father Gannon deserves great praise. Prior to 1947 Jesuits doing graduate work were spread out all over the campus. They had little community life. With the opening of Spellman Hall they were brought under one roof with a community chapel, dining facilities, and recreation rooms.

They were all young Jesuits, numbering fifty, either priests or scholastics, relatively early in their Jesuit careers, studying for masters or doctoral degrees and preparing for their future apostolic work in education. They came from every Jesuit province in the United States as well as from Canada, South America, the Philippines, the various countries of Europe, from India and other nations. All this made for a good exchange of ideas, information, and viewpoints. In addition, they were able to engage in a community life of liturgy and prayer, which is so essential for a Jesuit.

There were days of recollection and tridua throughout the year, and occasionally the entire community would go off to a retreat house for liturgy, prayer, and discussion. When all this is considered, it can be seen that Spellman Hall was a source of great spiritual and intellectual strength for the Society of Jesus. Many of its members went on to be Jesuit Provincials and rectors, presidents, administrators, and teachers in Jesuit universities and high schools all over the world. Some have been closely connected with Fordham University.

Father Michael Walsh was a member of the first community in 1947, studying for his doctorate in biology. He was later to become President of Boston College and after that President of Fordham. Father Joseph O'Hare,

currently President of Fordham, lived at Spellman Hall while completing his doctorate in philosophy during the 1960s. I myself was a member of the first community in 1947 as a scholastic, studying philosophy. As a priest I returned as Superior of Spellman Hall from 1962 to 1967. It was then turned into a residence hall for women. So I have the dubious distinction of having been a member of the first and last Jesuit community of Spellman Hall.

Several factors led to its conversion to a student dormitory. First in 1964 a new college for women was begun on the Rose Hill campus, called Thomas More College. There was a need for separate boarding facilities for women. At the same time, there existed on campus the Messenger of the Sacred Heart building, its staff, administrative offices, and printing press being located in what is now Murray–Weigel Hall, named for two well-known Jesuits. For various reasons, the Messenger of the Sacred Heart decided to move its operation downtown. As a result its building was completely renovated as a residence, and the Jesuits moved there from Spellman Hall. In the fall of 1967, Spellman Hall opened its doors to women boarders.

REV. ELBERT RUSHMORE, s.j.

Rev. Elbert Rushmore, s.j., earned his master's degree from Fordham's Graduate School of Arts and Sciences in 1950 and his Ph.D from the School of Education in 1969. He has been a member of the Theology Department faculty since 1952.

I came to Fordham as a Jesuit priest in 1952 and was assigned to the Theology Department. The Theology Department in 1952 was at the beginning of a series of changes which took place during the next 15 or 20 years. Before this period, college theology was pretty much seminary theology in English. In the late '40s, educators in our Jesuit New York Province, the late John Courtney Murray in particular, began to realize that for college students who were members of the laity, and would be members of the laity all their lives, it was not adequate just to have a seminary course in English.

In 1952 Fordham was making the first moves of breaking away from that mode. The Chairman of the Theology Department at that time was Father John Dwyer, s.j., and he had worked out a course for senior year. That is what I taught in the school year 1952–1953. It was pretty much dogmatic theology, particularly concerned with God and the universe, God as Creator.

The next step I remember in Fordham's evolving Theology Department was the introduction of a series of books by Father John Fernan; he was another Jesuit. As a seminarian, he had worked with Father John Courtney Murray. Father Fernan worked out a program based on the Gospels. I might remark that this was before the "new look," the new Catholic interpretation of Scriptures, got to the shores of the United States. His series is based on a view of the Gospels which is no longer held: namely, the view that the Gospels were good history without much interpretation by the authors. So, the course built on his four textbooks lasted only six or eight years.

Looking back from the vantage point of the new understanding of Scripture, you would have to say that this course had a fatal flaw, inasmuch as it was based on a view of Scripture which is no longer held and really is not tenable: the Gospels as history books. However, I think Father Fernan deserves great credit because he was a pioneer, and the course was aimed at lay students. It also was based on Scripture, an attempt to make much more use of Scripture in the theology course than hitherto.

The next change in undergraduate theology I recall had to do with the freshmen theology course and here the pioneer was Father Augustine Grady, who is now an emeritus member of the Theology Department. He was instrumental in bringing into the Department a course which was adapted to the 1960s. It was a course which emphasized Existentialism, taking that as a starting point. Existentialism was very much in vogue in philosophical and theological circles of that era, and he introduced us to that and also to the study of comparative religion.

Another major change took place in the '70s, and here the leader was Father Robert Roth, s.J., who was Dean of Fordham College. He was instrumental in working out, or leading the faculty in working out, the core curriculum that is still in use in Fordham College. Father Roth's concern was not only the Theology Department but all the academic departments. The project, which was worked out with many faculty members contributing, was part of a national movement of "back to basics."

In the period of the '60s, there had been unrest on campus and also academically there was a feeling we had to get rid of all the old things and start a fresh curriculum. By the early '70s, the deficiencies of that attitude were clear, and the feeling across the country was "return to basics." Under Father Roth's direction, the entire undergraduate curriculum, theology included, was revised.

Another great change in theology at Fordham was the institution of the graduate program in theology which led to the conferring of the master's degree and the doctorate in theology. Here the great credit goes to the late Father Robert Gleason, s.J. Father Gleason was the one who really convinced the administration that this should be done, and who worked very hard to bring the graduate program into existence. Now the Theology Department, like the other departments in the University, has its graduate division.

When I first joined the Department in 1952 it was composed of Jesuits plus one Carmelite priest. Now, of course, the Theology Department has lay men and lay women, and it also has members who are not Catholic. Also, as in any other department in the University, a person would not even be considered to join the Department unless he or she has the doctorate.

I think we can say that theology departments in Catholic colleges and universities now are academically respectable. They are on the same level as the programs in the humanities: philosophy, modern languages, history, sociology. The battle has been won.

REV. ROBERT J. SEALY, s.j.

Rev. Robert J. Sealy, s.j., a 1939 graduate of Fordham College, taught French in the Department of Modern Languages for more than 30 years, beginning as an Instructor in 1945. Father Sealy was Chairman of the Department from 1967 to 1973 and from 1979 to 1981.

My father was one of the founding members of the Fieldston Corporation, a closed community that was in the North Bronx. When I lived there, there were only two Catholic families, and the tradition was not to send their children to the Jesuits but to the Irish Christian Brothers at All Hallows.

The Christian Brothers are very strong in languages, and I did very well in French there. As a result I did very well in French when I came to Fordham Col-

lege. When I entered the Society of Jesus, I took a master's degree in French. Then, after studies in the Society, I was all set, since I was clever in my studies, to go to Rome when the Provincial said, "No, go to Paris and take your Ph.D." So I came back and taught French at Fordham.

By that time the graduate program had come to its full maturity. The Graduate School of Arts and Sciences had been introduced some years earlier by Father Robert Gannon, Fordham's President. One very specific reason, according to Father Gannon's thinking, was that there was no graduate school of quality which could service the many brothers and nuns who were teaching in the City and State of New York. He felt we had to put money and time into a good graduate program which would serve the group, the Catholics, who at that time were a minority, for whom the Jesuit schools had been founded to serve.

In the Modern Languages Department, the important people taught both graduate and undergraduate courses. The well-known scholars were the medievalists, John Misrahi and Fernand Vial. Dr. Misrahi was an American and Dr. Vial was Provençal. Both were excellent teachers and both published extensively. One reason Dr. Vial was so important at the time was because he was the official representative of the Cultural Embassy in New York for all university personnel from France in the United States. To have this French representative in your department is very important for the University and the University world.

The student enrollment numbers for the graduate programs in those days were very high because we had three programs: Spanish, French, and Italian. Unfortunately, Italian was on its way out and is now gone. We had a doctoral program in French and Italian and a master's program in Spanish. On the graduate level, we would have between 25 and 30 students in every class. One reason was that every summer Dr. Vial ran a program for the nuns which also fed into the Graduate School during the year.

After teaching for many years, I eventually became Chairman for eight years and during that time the numbers were very good. Gradually we increased the quality of our teaching staff. In the beginning, aside from a few key figures who controlled policy, we did not really have scholarly types teaching in all languages. Teachers in German and Italian were mostly confined to the College, but *petit à petit* we began to bring in reputable publishing scholars.

The first one I can remember who came in was John Pappas, who was an eighteenth-century specialist. After him we got André Vielwahr for the twentieth century and then Craig Brush for Renaissance. I was seventeenth and nineteenth century for my entire career.

While I was chairman we increased the personnel for the master's program in Spanish. We wanted to get a Ph.D program in Spanish, but that was impossible because of the beginning decline of student personnel. The reason for that decline was that when the Second Vatican Council opened up the schools to a less ghetto-like mentality, the nuns and brothers and priests whom we had taught and formed now quite rightly felt that they should, or could, attend secular universities. As a result, we were facing competition from NYU and Columbia and then, before we knew it, we had the State University of New York, or SUNY.

My philosophy as a teacher has always been that, in the beginning of the year, if students hate you you're lucky because they are going to work for you. At the end, they love you because you made them work. And that carries over to directing a dissertation. When a person is a certain age and wants to get a dissertation through, they want somebody who is going to push them to its conclusion, as rapidly as possible.

GEORGE F. SEUFFERT

George F. Seuffert has been Director of the Fordham University Band since 1951.

I had just come back from Marine Corps service and I heard that Captain Hoff, who was the conductor of the Fordham Band, had died. So, wanting to get involved in higher education, and having a tremendous amount of respect for Fordham, I wrote a letter to the Dean—Thurston Davis, I believe—giving him my background, saying I had been conducting bands since 1928. Within a week or two I was asked to come up to Fordham. Father Davis explained that they wanted their new conductor to conduct a rehearsal of the band, which I thought was quite logical and reasonable.

That was the first time I met Father Harold Mulqueen. I was tremendously impressed. He said to me, "Well, Mr. Seuffert, have you brought your music?" I said, "What music?" He said, "Every candidate who has come to apply for this position has brought his music and given it out to the bandsmen for rehearsal." I said, "That really isn't necessary. Is there any program you contemplate doing within the next few weeks or so?" "Oh yes," he said, "We have a concert scheduled in Philadelphia." Father Mulqueen was a little nonplussed when I offered to take the band through that repertoire.

Father Davis was there and the band was a little rough at the beginning, but after 10 or 15 minutes they started to gel as a unit and I was delighted. Afterward, Father Davis said, "I liked what you did, but we have another candidate to hear from, a Father Ziemack from Cardinal Hayes High School." "Well," I said, "Father Davis, it's a great pleasure knowing you." I happened to know that Father Ziemack was a great friend of Cardinal Spellman's and I didn't think George Seuffert could meet that competition. However, within a week I was offered a contract and I took over the band immediately. That was the only contract I've ever had in my 38 years with the Fordham Band.

Father Mulqueen was just something special. He always had the interests of those young men

175

at heart. Then the inevitable happened: young ladies applied for membership in the Band. I'll never forget Father's reaction! There's still a picture in the Band Room of the boys standing around the table, grinning from ear to ear, and Father signing up this young lady for the Band and Father's expression was, "I guess I have to do it, but I don't have to like it."

If every band in the university world would receive the same support that the Fordham Band receives, they'd be very fortunate. Father McGinley was the President at the time I became Bandmaster and his support was phenomenal. Every President of the University I have worked with, including Father O'Hare, has known what the band means to the University from a cultural point of view. They know what it means that the students can continue their music, playing for the pleasure of playing, which is what I stress because I know that so few of them will ever consider becoming professional musicians.

Student participation has remained rather steady over the years. We've had bands as large as 60 or 65 occasionally and some-times in the forties. But now the band remains around 50 members each year. Of course, our big problem is always to maintain a good blend of instrumentation because instruments sort of come in cycles. You'll have years when you have a large trombone section and then suddenly they disappear and we have a large flute or clarinet section.

The Band has always taken part in a lot of civic functions. In the days of Father Mulqueen, when St. Patrick's Day was a holiday, the Band played in the parade every year. For the past 30 years the Band has played in New York's famous Steuben Day Parade, the German-American parade. Now they perform on Columbus Day in the Bronx. I don't think anything can take the thrill away from the youngsters who performed in the receptions or the welcoming parades for the American Olympic stars of a few years ago, or the World Series parades when the Yankees and the Mets have won the World Series.

When Father Mulqueen became incapacitated around 1983, he was named "Moderator Emeritus" and Rev. George McMahon, s.j., became Band Moderator, continuing band tradition.

RICHARD SEXTON

Dr. Richard Sexton is an Associate Professor Emeritus in the Department of English.

This Sesquicentennial Celebration of Fordham marks my own 66th anniversary of association with the University which began with my entrance into the Preparatory School in February 1925. My degrees—B.A. (1932), M.A. (1935), and Ph.D (1965)—are all Fordham. My appointment to the faculty of Fordham College, Manhattan Division, in September 1935 marked the start of my career in six Fordham schools, a career which continued until my retirement in 1977 as Associate Professor of English Emeritus. By that title I will retain my professional association with Fordham for the rest of my life. My longest service was in the undergraduate School of Business in which I chaired the Department of English and Speech from 1949 to 1962, and was faculty moderator of the student newspaper, *The Maroon Quill,* and the yearbook, *The Aries.*

In 1965, a major reorganization of the humanities program brought about my transfer to the English Department of Fordham College at Rose Hill. There I was welcomed as an undergraduate professor in my own Alma Mater, assigned my own private office which overlooked the "elm-lined path," which was so familiar to me from my days at Fordham Prep. In that same year, a major professional improvement in my own identity was the award, in course, of the Ph.D degree.

My doctoral dissertation, directed by Dr. Grover Cronin, was a study of the American critic Yvor Winters, who was then a professor at Stanford University. This study, which would be expanded to include Winter's later work, was recommended for publication by the American editor of Mouton, Professor C. H. van Schoonvald of Indiana University. The book, entitled *The Complex of Yvor Winter's Criticism,* appeared in 1973, published by Mouton in Paris and The Hague. It was the second of two scholarly monuments based on my doctoral thesis. The first was my scholarly address "On the Relation of the Creative

Writer to Reality," delivered at the Tenth World Congress of the International Federation of Modern Languages and Literatures, at the University of Strasbourg in France, on September 1, 1966. A review of the book by the internationally known critic Denis Donohue appeared on page 1 of the *Times Literary Supplement* on August 30, 1974.

It once was observed that memory clings to each leaf that it saves. In the life of a professor the leaves are surely too many for a brief oral history sketch. I feel that I must note with pride and gratitude my two awards of Fordham University's Bene Merenti Medals for twenty and forty years of service respectively; the appreciative scroll awarded by the Department of Education of the Archdiocese of New York, in St. Patrick's Cathedral on June 22, 1972, for "thirty-five years of dedicated service"; and, as a symbolic memento of all my many thousands of Fordham students, a bronze plaque with wishes for a "job well done through the years" from the School of Business, Class of 1941. Now, in 1991, on Fordham's Sesquicentennial, as a Emeritus Associate Professor, I am happily in my 66th successive year at Fordham, perhaps a record among the living.

Deo gratias!

BERNARD M. SHANLEY

Photo by Pach Bros., N.Y.

Bernard M. Shanley is a 1928 graduate of Fordham Law School and a partner in the Morristown, N.J., law firm of Shanley & Fisher. A graduate of Columbia University, Mr. Shanley served as an adviser to President Dwight D. Eisenhower, holding such positions as Deputy Chief of the White House Staff, Special Counsel and Secretary to the President.

The School of Law

I had a wonderful time at Fordham, in no small measure because of Senator Eddie O'Mara, from Jersey City, who taught New Jersey Practice. He was a great friend of John Loughram, Chief Judge of the Court of Appeals, who also taught Evidence at Fordham Law. Loughram was a lovely man and a wonderful person.

They very kindly used to have me for dinner every Friday night, which was when they taught. Those sessions taught me a lot about the law, but I was also fascinated with the law profession because both of these men were great individuals in addition to being great lawyers. Like my father, I expected to go into business. But Eddie O'Mara, who knew my father and who knew how my father wanted me to get a law degree, said, "Bern, you ought to practice law. What do you want to go into business for?" And so I succumbed.

At Fordham, I also greatly enjoyed Maurice Wormser's course on Corporations. He was a very interesting fellow and an excellent teacher. I remember one time I was working pretty hard at the game. We had an exam and I cited two or three cases as answers to the question and Wormser got up and said, "You know, I can understand some of these people knowing the answers to all my questions, but I don't understand why somebody cites a case for an answer—and it's a correct case and answer. I gave him an A+. That's Mr. Shanley." I had to laugh. He was very cute about it.

Life with Ike

I was asked to help run the 1952 campaign. My wife, Maureen, agreed to it and so I did. In fact, I handled the delaying action for Eisenhower without which he would never have been nominated for the presidency by the Republicans. A group of Senators, Congressmen, and Governors was called to a meeting in south Jersey at the home of Amos Peasley. Governor Duff of Pennsylvania was there, as were Governors Sherman Adams of New Hampshire and Thomas Dewey of New York. They all wanted Eisenhower nominated because they thought Taft couldn't win against the Democrats, who would be nominating Adlai Stevenson.

The meeting, at Peasley's home in Clarksboro, took place on one of the hottest weekends the world has ever known. It was so hot we could hardly sleep. After three days we concluded that unless Senator Robert Taft from Ohio was taken on in the primaries, he would be nominated and we would lose the election. So during almost all of 1951 I traveled the country and led the way for opposing Taft in the primaries. Warren Burger, who would later become Chief Justice of the United States, was my deputy.

We recruited Harold Stassen to be the stalking horse, which created a problem with Governor Dewey, who was a political opponent of Stassen's. I went to Dewey and asked him if he'd let Stassen be the stalking horse. Dewey didn't know me very well, but he looked me in the eye and said, "You know, Mr. Shanley, we trust you, but we don't trust

Harold Stassen." Dewey was afraid Stassen would want to become more than a stalking horse. But eventually Dewey agreed because he knew Stassen was a good campaigner. I went to Stassen and, fortunately, he agreed to do it. He didn't get very many votes, but he did pull votes away from Taft to Eisenhower and so our strategy worked.

I got to be very close to Eisenhower because I lived with him night and day during that '52 campaign. We dragged him out of bed and put him to bed. We'd come back from campaigning at night and we'd all sit down and have a drink together and go to bed.

After the campaign, Eisenhower said to me, "Bern, what are we going to do with Henry Cabot Lodge?" And I said, "The perfect place for him, Mr. President, is at the United Nations. He'll stick his nose in the air and the Russians won't know what to make of it." It worked beautifully. He was perfect up there. The Russians didn't know how to handle him.

When it came time for Eisenhower to take over, he asked me if I would become Secretary of the Army. But we had three young kids at the time and Maureen was against it. She said, "You've done your part. You gave up '51 and you ran with him in the campaign. Forget it." Ike was very disappointed because he thought Secretary of the Army was next to being President. It was the number two job in the world. He was also disappointed because we had become very close friends. He said to me, "Bern, if I don't see you for ten years, our relationship would still be the same." That's how it was. A short time later he offered me the job of Deputy Chief of Staff and Special Counsel, which I accepted. "You can't refuse," Maureen said.

Washington was a lovely town to be in. Maureen was reluctant to go at first, but after we lived there she didn't want to leave. We had many good friends there. Years later people would ask when I returned if I missed the glamour. What glamour? I started to work on Monday morning and before I knew it it was Friday night. It was 17 hours a day and every fifteen minutes there was another crisis. Still, it was a remarkable experience.

Life with Gehrig

As a student at Columbia College, I played on the baseball team. I began as a pitcher but after I hit a home run one day, our coach moved me to third base. I didn't know the first baseman, but I remember the first time he threw the ball from first to third. I saw how hard the ball was coming and I knew if I caught it I'd end up in the bleachers. But I also knew if I didn't catch it I'd be called a sissy. I caught it.

Later, I said to the first baseman, "Where did you get that arm? You almost knocked me into the bleachers." His name was Lou Gehrig. We became fast friends and roommates. We were inducted into the Phi Delta Theta fraternity together. He was an exceptional person who did a great deal for baseball. Kids loved him and with good reason.

MICHAEL SHEAHAN

Michael Sheahan joined the Fordham staff in 1957 and was the University Secretary from 1968 until his retirement in December 1990. During that period, he was Executive Secretary of the Fordham University Council (1967–1979), the Board of Lay Trustees (1958–1969), and the Board of Trustees (1969–1990).

Early in 1958, the first serious effort to establish an advisory group of laymen to counsel and assist the University was made by Rev. Laurence J. McGinley, s.j., the 26th President of Fordham, and his fellow administrators.

In mid-June 1958, Father McGinley addressed letters to a number of prominent laymen explaining his intention to form such an advisory body. Eighteen persons responded to his invitation and became the nucleus of the Board of Lay Trustees. An organizational meeting was held at the University Club, in Manhattan, on the evening of June 30, 1958. Five of the original 18 members were graduates of Fordham University School of Law, two (including one of the five Law graduates) were graduates of Fordham College, and one man was a Fordham Prep alumnus. Fourteen of the 18 were then or subsequently recipients of honorary degrees from Fordham University.

There were 17 Catholics on the Board and one Protestant. The Protestant, Mr. George H. Cooper, was elected the first Chairman.

The Fordham University Council was proposed as a possibility on February 15, 1967, at a meeting of the Executive Committee of the Board of Trustees at the University Club, New York City. The proposal was presented by the Vice President for University Relations, Robert A. Kidera.

To broaden the base of volunteer support and participation in the development of the University, Mr. Kidera proposed that a body be formed to be called "The Fordham University Council." This would be a large group of 200 people or so, to be nominated by the Trustees, who would lend additional prestige and stature to the University. The group would be brought on campus for a full day of indoctrination and exposure, and additional workers would be recruited from this nucleus.

The matter was discussed at the March 15, 1967, meeting of the Board of Trustees and the formation of the Council was approved by the Trustees. The Council's first annual meeting was held at Rose Hill on November 4, 1967. There was an afternoon conference, which included two panel discussions, and there was a formal business meeting later in the afternoon.

A constitution and by-laws for the Council were approved. Officers were elected: Chairman, Mr. Felix E. Larkin, of W. R. Grace & Co.; Vice-Chairman, Mr. Robert B. Beusee, of WOR Radio–TV; Mr. William F. Leonard, of Olin Mathieson Chemical Corporation; and Mr. Joseph K. Mikita, of Westinghouse Broadcasting Co., Inc. Appointments to the Administrative Board of the Council were also approved for: Mr. F. Clay Buckhout, of Time, Inc.; Mr. Edgar Debany, of Lisanne, Inc.; and Mr. Robert J. Whalen, of Shields and Company. After the business meeting, there was a reception and dinner.

In its existence, the Council had five Chairmen in addition to Mr. Larkin. They were Mr. Mikita; Mr. Edward I. O'Brien, who now heads the Securities Industry Association, but who had been associated with Bache & Co. earlier; Dr. Vincent F. Guinee, now of Houston, Texas, but then associated with the New York City Department of Health in an executive capacity; Mr. Charles E. Murphy, who was a Vice-Chairman of Korn/Ferry, an executive recruiting firm; and the late Henry H. Salzberg, an attorney-at-law.

In a press release dated December 17, 1968, Fordham University announced a reorganization of its leadership structure and an enlargement of its Board of Trustees to give laymen a majority. Under the reorganization, which was to become effective on January 21, 1969, Rev. Leo McLaughlin, s.j., President of Fordham since 1965, would become its Chancellor, a newly created post. His primary responsibility was to be the development of support to meet the financial needs of the University.

Rev. Michael P. Walsh, s.j., who earlier in 1968 had resigned as President of Boston College after ten years in that office, was to become Fordham's new President. Father Walsh had been Chairman of Fordham's Board of Trustees.

At the same time, Mr. Joseph A. Kaiser, President of the Williamsburgh Savings Bank, was to become Chairman of the Board of Trustees. Mr. Kaiser had been Chairman of the University's Board of Lay Trustees, a group of laymen who had met with and advised the legal Board of Trustees, which had been made up exclusively of Jesuit priests. Mr. Kaiser was one of 15 laymen added to the nine-member Board.

The first meeting of the reconstituted Board of Trustees took place after luncheon at the Lotos Club in New York City on February 5, 1969. Of the 17 new trustees, ten had served on the former Board of Lay Trustees and two were members of the Fordham University Council. Thirteen of the 26 members were educators; eight were from business, banking, and industry; 13 had earned doctoral degrees; and 12 were Fordham alumni.

By the end of the 1990 academic year, 86 meetings of the Board of Trustees have been held since 1969. (I might say I have attended, to date, 85 meetings.) In that time 119 persons have served as trustees: 57 of them Fordham alumni, 38 of them Jesuits, 81 lay persons, including nine women; and the meetings have been presided over by the following Chairmen in the order of their service: Joseph A. Kaiser, Felix E. Larkin, George E. Doty, Richard J. Bennett, Thomas F. X. Mullarkey, and Thomas F. Kane. Nineteen of the 119 have been awarded honorary Fordham doctorates.

NORMAN O. SMITH

Dr. Norman O. Smith began his 34-year teaching career at Fordham in 1950 as an Associate Professor of Chemistry. He was appointed Professor in 1965 and was Chairman of the Chemistry Department from 1974 to 1978. He was named a Professor Emeritus in 1984.

By 1950 I had been for 11 years on the staff of the University of Manitoba in Winnipeg, Canada, and I saw an ad in *Chemical and Engineering News* for a position at Fordham. I came down for an interview, was hired, and started that September. Father McGinley was President at the time; Father Gisel was Chairman of the Department. I always said that the fact that my wife's name was O'Connor had something to do with my being hired here.

In those days, the cafeteria was in the basement of Keating Hall and I remember, as an Episcopalian trying to get a ham sandwich on a Friday, being nudged by the person next to me in line that they discouraged that. . . . We were asked to open classes with either three Hail Mary's or one Lord's Prayer. Being an Episcopalian, I chose the Lord's Prayer.

It was the custom here for the lecturer to say the first half of the Lord's Prayer and the class to respond by saying the second half. I would say the first half rather deliberately and the second half was rattled off at great speed much to my annoyance. After a while I couldn't take this, and I requested the class to say their part as deliberately as I said my part. We got along fine for a few days, but eventually the second half got faster and faster and we were back in no time to where we started. And that was the end of the efforts of an Episcopalian to change things at Fordham.

The Chemistry Department was structured like any other department, generally. I wasn't aware of any sharp delineation between undergraduate and graduate work because some of us taught in both, some of us did not. Hiring and firing was done behind the scenes, as was true in most departments. It was done by the chairmen and the administration with little input from ordinary faculty members.

When I arrived there were several strong faculty members, including men like Cerecedo, Brown, Hennessy, and Nord. There was also a chemist named Tibor Laszlo, who had come here from Hungary. He was a very capable person, and we became good friends. But what most people didn't know about our Department was that we had a solar furnace on campus. It consisted of a Navy search light, many feet in diameter, which was located just east of what is now Finlay Hall. At the focus of the reflecting mirror the sun's rays converged and we recorded temperatures of several thousand degrees. Tibor Laszlo was the man responsible for the solar furnace, which made Fordham unique for a time. Like Fordham's seismograph, the furnace attracted people from all over the world.

Physical Chemistry at Fordham had traditionally been a weak spot and I was given to understand that one reason I had been hired in the first place was to try to rectify that. Physical Chemistry, along with Inorganic Chemistry, Organic Chemistry, Analytical Chemistry, and Biochemistry, are the different branches of the science that blend into one another.

The old Chemistry Building was very old. It was crowded, and the plumbing was disintegrating. I had an office on the third floor that was veritably a Turkish bath in the winter. The Physical Chemistry laboratory in the basement was constantly being flooded from rain. Somehow we managed—perhaps because occasionally we were led to believe that things were going to get better.

Physical Chemistry requires rigorous thinking in mathematics, and for a department lacking in that discipline to a great extent, it was tough going trying to build it up, especially since Organic Chemistry students were in the majority. The science students, with some exceptions, had poor mathematics backgrounds.

At a university like Fordham, which has such a strong liberal arts program, there is always some difficulty in finding enough hours to give a good course in chemistry for four years. By contrast, at a school like M.I.T. or any other school with a strong chemistry department, it is often the case that students are kept so busy with their major that there is a minimum of time available for liberal arts. Fordham won't stand for that, of course, and I can understand that. So we've always lived in a situation where we squeeze in as much chemistry as the traffic will bear.

There is no question that a scientist's life is greatly enhanced by some sort of exposure to the humanities. Whether that exposure only at the college level comes too late in their lives to be of any use, I'm uncertain. But I happen to be a church organist as a sideline and my interest in music is certainly something that has greatly enhanced my life. (I have a son who is a professional cellist.) Indeed, there is a certain parallel between music and science. Bach's music is riddled with mathematical implications, although they are not obvious on first hearing. But the beauty of music is something that stands on its own.

I succeeded Dr. Franck as Chairman of the Department in 1974. I devoted most of my energies during my four years to trying to get our Ph.D. program approved by New York State, and in doing so, we built up a fine department—16 professors, including Dr. Weber, who was a dual member of the Physics and the Chemistry departments. We had several hundred thousand dollars in grants and we had the physical plant. Our graduate students were average, but something went wrong and we lost our Ph.D. program. Some of us feel that more evidence of financial support from the administration would have led to a different outcome. I have to say this was one of the saddest days in the history of our Department.

REV. CHARLES TAYLOR, S.J.

Rev. Charles Taylor, S.J., came to Fordham in 1951 after spending eight years as principal of Regis High School in Manhattan. At Fordham, he taught philosophy in the College of Pharmacy and he served as the Religious Superior of Spellman Hall, the Jesuit Scholastic residence.

Before the College of Pharmacy was formed in 1914, Fordham had a Medical School. When the Medical School was closed, the facilities of Thebaud Hall were used to begin the College of Pharmacy. At that time, it was predominantly Jewish in its clientele, and the definition I gave of philosophy precluded me from bringing in theology as an argument in the course. All students, regardless of their religion, had to take this course. But those who were not Catholic did not

have to take the course in religion. I taught this philosophy from 1951 to 1966.

One year after I arrived, in 1952, I was assigned by Father Laurence McGinley, who was President–Rector, to be Regent of the College of Pharmacy. That meant on Thursday morning, when the President–Rector held the weekly meeting for all the colleges at the University, I represented Pharmacy since no one but Jesuits were allowed and our Dean was a layman, Dr. Kidder. This of course was radically different from the current practice. The Regent was also accountable for the spiritual ministries of the College, confessions, distributing palms and ashes, as well as hearing anything the students wanted to tell me in confidence.

I was not aware of any conflict at all on any point of religion during my time. We had our Chanukah–Christmas party, usually off the campus in one of the neighboring restaurants. Much before Vatican II, back in 1914 when the College began, the first Dean who served for about 25 years was Jacob Diner, who was Jewish. As the years went on, and just before I left in 1966, the student body was predominantly Catholic, especially Italian Catholics. We began all classes with a prayer. I explained to the students, if you're not a Catholic you don't have to say the prayer, but you can't interfere with the

Catholics who are saying the prayer.

During my years there, we honored all the Jewish holidays. We also had an annual Catholic retreat of three days every year. We would bring in a lecturer for the non-Catholics who did not attend the retreat, a kind of equity gesture. These students were required to attend those lectures.

During my 15 years in Pharmacy, I had no direct contact with either the faculty or the student body of Fordham College. My only connection would be whatever was discussed on those Thursday morning meetings. There was an indifference to the College of Pharmacy on the part of the faculty and student body

of the Fordham College. It wasn't animosity, it was just that they didn't know what was happening with us.

I don't remember the exact date, but Dr. Kidder, our Dean, went into the Army and we needed a replacement. I asked Father McGinley to appoint Dr. Sica, who was teaching chemistry, and he did.

In August of 1966, my Provincial, the head of the New York Province of the Jesuits, sent me to be Rector of what we call 84th Street. It included the parish of St. Ignatius, Regis High School, Loyola School, and the Seminary and Mission Bureau. Shortly after I left, Fordham began to close the College of Pharmacy. No one was appointed Regent after I left.

REV. ANDREW VARGA, S.J.

Rev. Andrew Varga, S.J. was a professor of philosophy at Fordham from 1955 until his retirement in 1988. He wrote two books on bio-ethics: On Being Human: General Principles of Ethics *and* Main Issues in Bio-Ethics.

Hungarian Jesuits

I was born in Hungary, was raised in Hungary, and I got my education, most of it, in Hungary. Then for my graduate education, including my doctorate in philosophy, I went to the Gregorian University in Rome. After that, I was supposed to return to Hungary, but in the meantime all the Jesuit houses had been seized by the Communist regime. One midnight, all the Jesuits were transported to concentration camps. Fortunately I was not in

Hungary at the time. Unfortunately, I wasn't able to go back to Hungary after getting my doctorate. I went to Canada, where I taught at Regis College for four years. In 1955, I came to Fordham University.

I was supposed to teach ethics and psychology in the School of Business, but as I was getting ready for my courses, I received a letter from the Father General of the Society of Jesus, Father Janssens, appointing me Provincial of the Dispersed Hungarian Province. My predecessor, Father Reiss, was in Canada at the time, so I went to Canada to gather his documents. On my return, my first visit was to the Provincial of the New York Province, Father Henneberry. I then went to Father Laurence McGinley, who was the President–Rector of Fordham. They offered their help in organizing the Hungarian Province and in assisting me in getting adjusted to university life in America.

About a year later I began to visit the 160 members of the Hungarian Province who were dispersed in some 36 countries around the world. Many of them were only young men studying for the priesthood. I had to direct their studies and their spiritual development and get them ready for their own ordination.

In the meantime, the turbulence in Hungary continued. In October 1956, when the Hungarian Revolution had been going on for a few days, we all had hopes that it would succeed. But as we know from history, the Russian troops turned back to Hungary, and Budapest was destroyed again, as it was at the end of World War II. We tried to organize the escape of the Jesuit Scholastics who could not continue their studies in Hungary. Some 25 of these young men successfully crossed the border. I had to visit them and had to place them in different parts of the world to continue their studies.

Back at Fordham, some of the faculty members were very helpful. I remember Father Walter Jaskievicz organized a mass for the Hungarians. After the defeat of the Hungarian Revolution, about 200,000 Hungarians left the country. Many of them came to the United States, including college students.

Fordham gave scholarships to 20 Hungarian students (ten men, ten women) among the group who came to Fordham. They were given full scholarships and even some pocket money, be-cause they had nothing to start with except a few small belongings. Father Yanitelli was in charge of their financial support here, and I looked after their psychological adjustment to American college life. Most of them did quite well and most of them finished their studies. Some are still in contact with me.

When I came to Fordham, I was the first Hungarian Jesuit here, but others came after me. At that time, the University and Father McGinley were very helpful in that a number of Hungarian Jesuits were invited to become members of the faculty. They include Father Hegyi in Biology, Father John Adams, who is a stronghold of Fordham downtown, and also Father Hejja, Father Babos, and Father Serei, who came as an anthropologist. As I frequently told the University President, we are very grateful for all the help and hospitality given to us. He always told us, "We are grateful to you for giving us so many good students and teachers."

VIVIENNE THAUL WECHTER

Dr. Vivienne Thaul Wechter has been the University Artist in Residence and Adjunct Professor of Interdisciplinary Teaching-Psychology of Creativity and Inter-Arts at Fordham since 1964. Beginning in 1953, Dr. Wechter has been the host of a popular weekly program on WFUV which began as "Students View the News" and was later restructured and renamed "Today's World."

I started at Fordham University in '53 and we created a special program for Fordham called "Students View the News." We had a panel of four students and a guest expert. The guest expert was always a very distinguished person in his or her field, heads of government, ambassadors, senators, really distinguished people, writers, and so forth. The students had to do some home-

work in order to really understand the field, the area of expertise.

One of my wonderful students was Charlie Osgood. Then he was Charles Wood. He was so outstanding. I could always depend upon him to really be prepared and to be knowledgeable and poised. I remember, I used to say to him, you're really going to make it. The format has changed and the name of the program now is "Today's World."

By 1961 we had developed the art gallery in what was then called the Campus Center. We got a wonderful space, a 20-by-40-foot gallery. The Administration was very cooperative, as was Captain Segal, who was the first director of the Campus Center. Father Vincent O'Keefe was President at that time. He was very supportive of our work, of our dreams, of our plans. You realize this was a totally new concept for Fordham. We had a wonderful gallery in the Campus Center for many years, until we built our Lincoln Center Campus, and then we decided we'd move our exhibition program down there because of its central location.

We have a regular program of year-round exhibits. We have one every month and we publish a brochure which goes out all over the country. We also have a large outdoor sculpture area on the Robert Moses Plaza, where we site two exhibitions a year, of monumental outdoor work.

Silk Hall was where I had my first studio. There were no facilities there for women. Fernando was the porter who handled the building and when I had to use the facilities, I had to use the Jesuits' facilities and he would stand guard. And then I had no water in my studio. There must have been something very challenging for me to stay here under such circumstances. I had to go and get water and I would walk around with my pail of water and brushes. Once somebody came up to me and said, "Oh hello, are you the new maid on campus?" That was wonderful. The challenge was in creating the ferment for new ideas in the contemporary multi-arts and the involvement of the University community.

In the late '60s there was a change, partly because women students came to campus in much greater numbers. When women and men are together in the same environment, something is bound to happen. So there was a dynamic freedom and a certain change in the atmosphere. That was good.

Very often as I start a new semester now I reflect, "Oh, in the 1960s and 1970s, the students were really dynamically interested in exploring ideas." For example, they'd come to my studio and maybe stay until midnight and I'd have to say okay, you know, let's call it quits, let's go. But they'd want to talk about things or they'd want to do ex-

perimental theater, or dance, or music.

I remember one night—we drove all around New York, I took them to Judson Poets Theater, at the Judson Church, then to Cafe La Mama, the experimental theater. And then they stopped at my home. When it was about 4:00 A.M. I said to them, "Listen, I have to be on campus at nine o'clock. It's late." They said, "Don't worry; we'll get you there at nine o'clock."

Today's students are more pragmatically oriented. But when I feel disheartened because they are not breaking down my studio door to come here and spend hours just talking and so forth, I get a wonderful surprise, like what happened at the end of last semester when we had so many wonderful creative productions using video and film.

In the late '60s we started a program of exhibitions in what we call the Lowenstein Library Gallery. We opted for that space for two reasons. One, we have no special separate museum gallery space and the next best was to have part of the library, where the architecture is such that we have 170 feet of wall space in the rear of the gallery; we also have a large central wall space for wall pieces, and the central area for sculptures, and the work is very safe there. There are many conferences that are held in the library and they do go to see the exhibits.

For exhibiting space we also

have, as I mentioned, the Robert Moses Plaza. It is a huge outdoor plaza. Perhaps it is not the most hospitable to art because it's so bare in a sense, but when we get good work together, it makes it very exciting. We've had very important artists like George Rickey, who was one of the originators of sculpture that is not powered by a motor, but just turns in the wind. We've had *Homage to New York*, and this was by the Israeli sculptor, one of the leading Israeli sculptors, Igael Umarkin, who came here and created sculptures at our request, specifically for our site.

People see the art, they enjoy it, but it reaches a deeper level of one's consciousness and development. So our art program is really very important not only to our University community, but to our surrounding community at large.

HONORABLE MALCOLM WILSON

Malcolm Wilson, the former Lieutenant Governor and Governor of New York, began his long association with Fordham in 1925 as a student at Fordham Prep. He graduated from Fordham College in 1933 and from the School of Law in 1936.

My experience at the Prep and the College was a definite factor in my decision to choose Fordham Law. Many of my classmates at Fordham College, instead of taking their senior year on campus at Rose Hill, came down to Fordham Law School and did the first year of law. If they completed their first year with satisfactory marks, they received their degree from the College. So, knowing many of those men who had done that and were pleased with the Law School firmed my own decision.

I attended the evening session of the Law School at Rose Hill. We started out with sixty students in September of 1933. Without exception, all of us were working some place. Many of the men were married, and all had jobs. We had policemen, school teachers, even subway guards. (In those days, you were lucky to get a job that paid $1500 dollars a year.) I found that very advantageous because everyone who was there was a serious student, and it was helpful to have the influence of those older men who were out in the world.

We had the same number of hours as the day students—12 hours a week. We had mainly an adjunct faculty up at Rose Hill. The full-time professors we did have were John'F. X. Finn, Gene Keefe, George Bacon, and Thomas L. J. Corcoran. Our only relationship with the downtown Law School was that we all took our examinations together at the end of each semester. And we were all together for graduation day.. My class was the second last class to attend school uptown because the year after I was graduated in 1936, night student applicants were required to go four years and the Law School enrollment plummeted. That's because you could still finish law school in three years at night at St. John's, Brooklyn Law School, and New York Law School.

Other than the *Law Review*, there was only one extra-curricular activity at Law School; that was the Saint Thomas Aquinas Sodality. The sole activity of the Sodality was to have three communion breakfasts a year on the campus. I was elected president of the group at the end of my second year. We used to have 200 or 250 people in attendance—and very faithful faculty members.

My experience would be rather different from that of present-day students. In the first place, there were no electives at all. You got what you took and you took what you got. Now there's a cafeteria, of course, 120 or so course offerings. We took Contracts, Torts, Real Property, Personal Property, Bills and Notes, Criminal Law, Wills, Equity, Evidence, Practice, and Pleadings. We took Jurisprudence for one semester.

It's a source of great joy to me that one of my daughters is a graduate of Fordham Law School. My late wife, Katharine, and I had just two daughters. In 1977, thirteen years after she got out of college, our elder daughter, Kathy, decided to go to Law School. Because she lived in New Rochelle with her husband, John Conroy, and four young sons, I expressed the view that Pace University Law School in White Plains would be easier to attend. However, because I had gone to Fordham, as well as three of her cousins who are lawyers, she drove down from New Rochelle

to Fordham Law School at Lincoln Center for three years. Son number five arrived in the summer between her first and second years at the Law School.

I never had a drink in my life. The reason is related to Fordham. When I went to Fordham College, my mother asked me, "I hope you won't smoke or drink at college." I was fifteen years old and said "O.K." When I got out of college, I was nineteen, and my mother said to me, "If you want to smoke, it's all right. Your father smokes, but I hope you won't drink while you're in law school." I said fine.

It was while I was in law school that Gene Fowler's book *The Great Mouthpiece* came out and became a bestseller. It was about Bill Fallon, a great trial lawyer, and when I read it, I saw too many parallels. He was Irish; I was Irish. He was a lawyer; I was studying law. He went to Fordham; I was in Fordham. He was interested in politics; I was interested in politics. And the poor guy died in the gutter of overindulgence in alcohol.

It was only two years later that I was elected to the State Legislature and went to Albany. Before World War II, Albany was vastly different from what it is today. There was a sort of devil-may-care attitude. Thank God, I could stay up with the best of them, but still get to the office the first thing in the morning.

CLASS OF 1929

Several members of Fordham College Class of 1929 recall their experiences at Rose Hill. They include Donald J. Ryan, Ed Durner, Tom Quinn, and John Fitzsimons.

DON RYAN: I have two things to mention. One is that I was a member of the first class that started the college experience in February. A new program was begun whereby people who got out of high school in January could come right in and go through the summer, and by September catch up to the class of '29 and become members of it.

We had Gabe Liegey as one of our teachers and, of course, he stayed with the University many, many years after that. Frank Grady taught Greek; Lloyd Manning taught Latin. Those were pleasant days, particularly in the summer when we would have class and then head for the indoor swimming pool below the gym.

Another thing that I remember with relish is the fact that I managed to become a member of the College band when we were performing for football games. One of the things that we did was to be taken up to Boston to see Fordham play against Boston College. We went on a night boat that took off from somewhere in Manhattan, sailed through Long Island Sound and pulled into some point in Rhode Island. Then we went by train up to Boston for the game. That was quite an adventure for us at that time, and it's an experience no longer possible.

ED DURNER: When we graduated, I got a job on Wall Street, and my boss was a very good friend of Father Dean. Father Dean used to go down to Staten Island every weekend and say Mass at my boss's church. So, when my boss heard that I came from Fordham, he called Father Dean and he said, "Have you any more boys up there?" So Father Dean sent Bob Purtell and Ray Hartigan down and the three of us all worked in the same brokerage house, and then came the crash in 1929. Ray Hartigan went on to become a member of the firm, and Bob Purtell, of course, was killed in World War II. I'm the only one here to say "Good Morning" to all of you.

TOM QUINN: The day of our graduation, I saw a beautiful open Packard pull up to the College and a gentleman, with a little assistance, got out and got up, and he gave the speech of the occasion for our graduation. I was very much impressed and said, "That man will go far." It's one of the few occasions in my life I've ever been right, and I can't forget it. His name was Franklin D. Roosevelt.

JOHN FITZSIMONS: We had Father Bunn—I think it was "Mr." then—over in the auditorium, teaching English. He gave us an assignment one weekend to come in with a poem. So, of course, everybody was back with a poem on Monday morning, reading it, getting approbation or a few comments. I read my poem and he said, "What's this?" I said, "That's poetic license." He said, "Who ever told you that you were a poet?"

DON RYAN: A few years after our class moved on, I came back to teach here at the College, and George Leonard, who was in the Class of '28, was well established on the faculty as a teacher of English. In those days, students who were to be football players first had to serve on the freshman team. One of those years, in the middle '30s, when our teams had nationwide stature in merit and esteem, the freshman team promised to become a real powerhouse in varsity ranks later on. However, they had to pass their subjects. There was one great end by the name of Steve Simonowicz who was having trouble with English and, sure enough, at the end of the first semester, he failed. As was the custom in those days, he was allowed to continue if he took a coaching course in the afternoon in the spring and made up the work.

George Leonard was given the job of giving him special tutoring and then the final exam. Those were the years when Pitt also was a great football power, and the great name on the Pittsburgh team in the backfield was Marshall Goldberg. Well, one day in the teachers' room, George Leonard was sitting there, looking at the final exam paper of the coaching course, and he looked at it, and he looked at it, and he said finally, "Steve should really fail, but every time I go to put the failing mark on it, I see Goldberg coming around the end."

P.S. Steve never played for Fordham and Goldberg never crossed the goal-line. Fordham and Pitt played three successive scoreless ties.

FORDHAM UNIVERSITY:
A CHRONOLOGY

1692	Original Rose Hill Manor House is built on approximately what is now the site of Collins Hall. Tradition has it that General George Washington and his staff used it for a time during the Revolution. It will serve as the college infirmary until its demolition in the 1890s.
1838	Present Rose Hill Manor House is built. It is now the central part of the Administration Building. It will have two one-story extensions, replaced in 1870 by the present north and south wings. Wings once extended out of the back of the building toward Keating Hall.
1838	John Hughes comes to New York as Coadjutor Bishop (Bishop, 1839; Archbishop, 1850) to the Most Rev. John Dubois and begins a search for a site to situate a seminary and a college.
1839	John Hughes purchases Rose Hill Manor, then a farm of about 100 acres, bordering on the Bronx River and including part of the present Botanical Garden, for about $30,000.
1840	Alumni House built. Believed to be the work of architect William Rodrique, it will serve as his family home during the construction of the adjacent church and residence hall. Rodrique was the brother-in-law of Archbishop Hughes.
1840	St. Joseph's Seminary opens at Rose Hill with approximately 14 transfers from LaFargeville and 7 new admissions. After it closes in 1859, the seminarians are sent to St. Joseph's Seminary, located first in Troy and later in Yonkers.
1841	June 24 (Feast of St. John the Baptist). St. John's College, as Fordham was first called, formally opens, with 6 students. The first President, John McCloskey, became the first Bishop of Albany, then Archbishop of New York, and later the first American Cardinal.
1845	The University Church, named for Our Lady of Mercy, is built. The stained glass windows, depicting the Four Evangelists and Sts. Peter and Paul, originally presented by King Louis Philippe of France to Bishop Hughes for use in old St. Patrick's Cathedral in downtown Manhattan, were found to be the wrong size for the Cathedral, and given to St. John's College, Fordham.
1845	Bishop Hughes and the Jesuits of the Province of France sign agreement whereby the Jesuits move the personnel of their

199

mission in Kentucky to New York and take over St. John's College at Fordham and, in 1846, St. Joseph's Seminary.

1846   April 10. The Governor signs an act granting St. John's College a university charter.

1846   July 15. The Jesuits begin to arrive from Kentucky; Bishop Hughes deeds the College over to the Jesuits for $40,000, but retains title to the seminary—about 9 acres—and the seminary buildings.

1847   July 18. *The New York Herald* publishes the following account of the 2nd commencement of St. John's College, held July 2, 1847: "All the regular trains of cars on the Harlem Rail Road were crowded during the morning, and at 1 o'clock p.m. an extra train of six cars was dispatched to take up passengers whose business or other engagements kept them in the city until that hour. . . . The exercises were conducted in a large tent erected for the occasion on the beautiful lawn in front of the College buildings. . . . There were present about two thousand persons, among whom we observed members of the City legislature, officers of the army and other public persons, besides hundreds of pretty girls, beautiful young ladies and good looking matrons. . . ."

1852   Our Lady of Mercy parish is organized. Services are celebrated in the college chapel, until Our Lady of Mercy Church was built in 1890 off campus.

1854   Debating Society established.

1855   First productions of St. John's Dramatic Society, *Henry IV* and *The Seven Clerks,* are staged.

1858   Institution of laboratory fees: $5 for the use of chemical apparatus.

1859   November 3. First regular baseball team is organized under the name of Rose Hill Base-Ball Club. The first college game in the United States with 9 on a side is played against St. Francis Xavier College, New York—33–11 in favor of Rose Hill.

1860   Archbishop Hughes signs deed of sale of seminary property over to St. John's College for $45,000.

1860   Alumni Association is founded.

1864   Gatehouse is built at Third Avenue and Fordham Road entrance as a test of the quality of stone from a local quarry. It will later be moved to its present site, assigned to the Honors Program, and renamed Alpha House.

1867   East section of what is now called Dealy Hall is built. The west front will be completed in 1891 and in 1935 the

	building will be named after Patrick F. Dealy, s.J., President from 1882 to 1885.
1874	Maroon selected as official college color.
1882	November. *The Monthly* begins publication.
1883	November 26. Football team organized. Their first game, against St. Francis Xavier, is lost 12–6.
1885	Military Cadet Battalion established.
1886	Science Building constructed. It will be renamed Thebaud Hall in 1935, after Augustus Thebaud, s.J., President of St. John's, 1846–1851 and 1860–1863.
1890	Present cemetery is opened, with removal of bodies from the first cemetery on property now belonging to The New York Botanical Garden. The last burial will occur in 1909.
1891	Second Division built. It will be named Hughes Hall in 1935, and will house Fordham Prep until 1972.
1891	June 24. A statue of the Founder, Archbishop John Hughes, is presented on the occasion of the 50th anniversary by the Fordham Alumni Association. In 1941 the site will be restored by the graduating class.
1893	December 4. The University Church, Our Lady of Mercy, is blessed and formally opened.
1897	Cap and gown introduced for Commencement.
1898	The Borough of the Bronx, which includes Fordham, is detached from Westchester County and annexed to New York City.
1902	Fordham plays its first intercollegiate basketball game, with Brooklyn Poly, and loses, 18–10.
1904	Collins Auditorium is built and named for John J. Collins, s.J., President from 1904 to 1906, and later Apostolic Vicar of Jamaica, B.W.I.
1905	September 28. Medical School opens in the Science Building (it will close in 1921); Law School, with 13 students and Paul Fuller as the first Dean, opens in Collins Auditorium.
1906	Law School moves to 42 Broadway. The case method of study introduced by Professor Ralph W. Gifford.
1907	An amendment to the original charter provides for the change of the corporate name from St. John's to Fordham University.
1907	Fordham University Press established. It is now housed in Canisius Hall, named for St. Peter Canisius, s.J.
1908	Law School moves to 20 Vesey Street with 146 students registered.

1910   First seismograph installed in basement of Administration Building by Father Edward P. Tivnan, S.J.

1911   New Medical School building completed. After the closing of the Medical School, the building becomes the Chemistry Building (later called the Old Chemistry Building and then New Hall. It will be named Finlay Hall in 1990).

1911   The Law School moves for the fourth time, to 140 Nassau Street. More than 400 students are registered.

1912   Evening Law School opens. John Whalen, who succeeded Paul Fuller, is named the first Dean.

1912   Carl Jung, the famous psychologist, delivers a course of lectures at the Medical School.

1912   College of Pharmacy established. It will close in 1971.

1913   Medical School moves to its new building, completed in 1911.

1914   *Fordham Law Review* founded. It will suspend publication in 1917 due to World War I.

1915   The 28th floor of the Woolworth Building becomes the home of the Law School for the next 28 years.

1916   November 6. Graduate School of Arts and Sciences, Teachers College, and School of Sociology and Social Service are organized and located in the Woolworth Building.

1916   June 12–14. Celebration of Diamond Jubilee, with more than 8,000 people in attendance.

1916   *The Maroon* is published for the first time.

1918   February 7. The first issue of *The Ram* is published.

1918   Students' Army Training Corps is initiated.

1920   The Department of Education of the Graduate School opens.

1920   The School of Business Administration opens as a School of Accounting.

1920   November 14. Stone pillars, which form Third Avenue Gate, are dedicated as gift of the Alumni Association. Memorial Plaques on gate will be added as gift of the Class of 1941.

1922   Erection of building for the *Messenger of the Sacred Heart*. It will be converted in 1965 into a residence for Jesuit scholastics and named Murray–Weigel Hall to commemorate two New York Jesuit theologians prominent in the days of Vatican II, John Courtney Murray and Gustav Weigel.

1923   Kohlmann Hall constructed as headquarters of the New York Province of the Society of Jesus and named for Anthony Kohlman, S.J., founder of the New York Literary Institution (1808–1814), the second Jesuit school in New York.

1923	Ignatius M. Wilkinson is named Dean of the Law School. He will serve in that capacity until his death in 1953.
1924	December 4. Construction of the University Gymnasium is completed.
1924	Seismic Observatory, donated by William Spain, is formally dedicated on the present site of Loyola Hall. It will be moved to the site of Keating Hall in 1927 and to its present site east of Freeman Hall in 1931.
1926	Duane Library is built and named for William J. Duane, S.J., President from 1924 to 1930.
1927	Larkin Hall (Biology Building) named for John Larkin, S.J., President from 1851 to 1854, is completed.
1928	Loyola Hall, named in honor of Ignatius Loyola, the founder of the Society of Jesus, is built to house the Jesuit faculty. Additional housing will be provided in 1960 in Faber Hall, named for Blessed Peter Faber, one of St. Ignatius' first companions.
1930	Freeman Hall (Physics Building), named after noted science teacher Thomas J. A. Freeman, S.J., opens.
1931	May 10. First annual Faculty Convocation. Seven faculty members and administrators are awarded the *Bene Merenti* medal.
1931	November 19. An amendment to the Charter of Fordham University provides for a change in the name of the Collegiate Department from St. John's College to Fordham College.
1932	First comprehensive examinations are held in the Graduate School.
1934	The School of Social Service is given its present title and expanded to offer graduate-level courses and degrees.
1935	*Fordham Law Review*, suspended due to World War I, resumes publication.
1936	May. The Law School receives provisional approval from the American Bar Association.
1936	Keating Hall, named for Joseph Keating, S.J., University Treasurer from 1910 to 1948, is completed. Though it was originally constructed for Seniors in Fordham College, its purpose is changed by Robert I. Gannon, S.J., who decides to house the Graduate School of Arts and Sciences there.
1936	Accreditation by the Association of American Law Schools is received.
1936	The Juniorate at St. Andrew-on-Hudson, Poughkeepsie (the first two years of college for Jesuit seminarians), is affiliated with Fordham College.

1936	The "Seven Blocks of Granite"—John Druze, Al Babartsky, Vincent Lombardi, Alex Wojciechowicz, Nat Pierce, Ed Franco, Leo Paquin—coached by the legendary "Sleepy" Jim Crowley, one of the "Four Horsemen of Notre Dame," dominate Fordham football.
1937	Association of American Universities admits Fordham to the circle of Universities of Complex Organization.
1938	August 1. Teachers' College merges with the Department of Education of the Graduate School to become the School of Education, offering both graduate and undergraduate instruction.
1938	Hilaire Belloc, English essayist, historian, novelist, journalist, and poet, is in residence in the History Department during the spring semester.
1938	Dr. Victor Hess, who had been awarded the Nobel Prize in Physics for his discovery of the cosmic rays, joins the Physics Department. He will teach until 1956.
1938	Thirteen red maple trees are donated by Class of '41 to form Constitution Row.
1939	A working model of Fordham's Seismic Station, designed by director J. Joseph Lynch, S.J., is the only individual university exhibit at New York World's Fair.
1939	The delegates of Pax Romana hold their first American Congress at Fordham.
1939	The quadrangle is renamed "Edwards Parade" at the unveiling of a memorial plaque to General Clarence Edwards, former commander of Fordham's Cadet Corps.
1940	St. John's Hall expands into Our Lady's Court (Queen's Court) with the construction of Bishops' Hall and St. Robert's Hall, named for Robert Cardinal Ballarmine, S.J.
1940	September 27. 400th Anniversary of the Society of Jesus. Celebration held in Keating Hall.
1940	Fordham assumes the publication of *Thought* from America Press.
1940–1941	September 28. Year-long Centennial Celebration begins, and Fordham Century Fund Appeal for $1,000,000 is launched.
1941	January 1. Fordham loses the Cotton Bowl against Texas A&M (13–12).
1942	January 1. Fordham wins the Sugar Bowl against Missouri (2–0).
1942	School of Social Service moves to 134 East 39th Street.
1942	The University Church hosts Archbishop Spellman at consecration of new reredos and triptych in connection with the

installation of its new altar. The inlaid marble altar, given in 1878 by diocesan clergy to St. Patrick's Cathedral, is donated to Fordham by Archbishop Spellman.

1943   With the $122,000 purchase of the Vincent Building at 302 Broadway, Fordham acquires a home for the School of Law, the School of Education, and Fordham College Manhattan Division.

1946   May 11. At the Charter Centenary on this date, President Harry S. Truman rings for the first time at Fordham the ship's bell of the Aircraft Carrier *Junyo*. The bell, presented by Admiral Chester W. Nimitz, is blessed by His Eminence Francis Cardinal Spellman as a memorial to "our dear young dead of World War II."

1946   Fordham institutes its Department of Communication Arts.

1947   October 26. At a special ceremony, WFUV is formally dedicated by Cardinal Spellman.

1947   Spellman Hall, named after alumnus Francis Cardinal Spellman, is opened to house Jesuit graduate students. The funds were contributed by the New York Province and Cardinal Spellman.

1948   May 23. The World War II Memorial in the University Church is dedicated by His Eminence Cardinal Spellman.

1948   Fordham Sigma Xi Club is formally installed.

1950–1951   The dormitories known as Martyrs Court are erected. They commemorate 'French Jesuits slain by the Iroquois on the Mohawk River in the 1640s: Isaac Jogues, René Goupil, and Jean Lalande.

1954   Football on a varsity level is dropped.

1954   Coffey Field is dedicated on the occasion of Jack Coffey's 33rd anniversary as baseball coach at Fordham.

1955   College of Philosophy and Letters, Shrub Oak, is affiliated with Fordham University. It will close in 1969.

1956   At the Olympic Games in Melbourne, Australia, Fordham's Tom Courtney wins the Gold Medal in 800-meter track competition.

1958   June 30. Organizational meeting of the Board of Lay Trustees.

1958   Fordham acquires approximately 320,230 square feet of property as a collegiate sponsor in the Lincoln Center Urban Renewal Project under Title 1 of the Housing Act of 1949. The acquisition cost the University $2,241,610. Acquisition of the Third Avenue El property also at this time.

1959   The Campus Center is constructed. It will later be named in honor of Laurence McGinley, s.J., President from 1949 to 1963.

1961	The nomadic existence of the Fordham Law School ends in 1961 when its new building is opened at Lincoln Center. The Attorney General of the United States, Robert F. Kennedy, speaks and is awarded an honorary degree.
1962	March 1. The official installation ceremonies of the Tau Chapter of Phi Beta Kappa are held.
1964	Club football is established.
1964	Thomas More College is created as a coordinate women's college. It will merge with Fordham College in 1974.
1964	The inception of women's basketball.
1965	The first meeting of the Faculty Senate. Dr. Joseph R. Cammarosano (FC '47) elected first president.
1966	September 14. First meeting of the combined Jesuit and Lay Boards of Trustees.
1966	Faculty Memorial Hall is converted from a five-story commercial loft building. It is rebuilt and renovated at a cost of $1,900,000. Plaques are placed in the lobby commemorating illustrious professors.
1966	A year-long observance of the 125th anniversary of the founding of Fordham University, with the theme "The University in the American Experience." Anniversary celebration culminates with an historic first visit to the United States by a Father General of the Society of Jesus, the Very Reverend Pedro Arrupe, S.J.
1966	April 5. Fordham University presents the Doctor of Laws Degree, *honoris causa,* to five men committed to worldwide religious liberty: Dr. Louis Finkestein, Reverend John Coleman Bennett, Most Reverend Archbishop Iakovos, Reverend Eugene Carson Blake, and the Reverend John Courtney Murray, S.J.
1967	Bensalem College, an experimental school, opens. It will close in 1974.
1967	Fordham is selected for the Albert Schweitzer Chair of Humanities. The chair is accepted by Dr. Marshall McLuhan of the University of Toronto.
1967	The Louis Calder Conservation and Ecology Study Center is acquired when the Louis Calder Foundation transfers the 115-acre estate to the University.
1968	November 16. John Mulcahy Hall named for the donor. The Chemistry Department moves there from the Old Chemistry Building.
1969	The Liberal Arts College at Lincoln Center is opened. All schools from 302 Broadway and 134 East 39th Street move

into the new facility, named for benefactor Leon Lowenstein.

1969   The Joseph A. Martino Graduate School of Business Administration, named for the trustee emeritus, is established at Lincoln Center.

1969   School of General Studies is developed out of the evening and adult programs, begun in 1944.

1969   February 5. First meeting of the Board of Trustees in its present form, including both laymen and Jesuits.

1970   February 19. New York State Education Department declares Fordham University qualified to receive Bundy Aid.

1970   Administration Building, St. John's Residence Hall, and Fordham University Chapel are designated Landmark Buildings by Landmarks Preservation Commission.

1972   Fordham Prep School moves from Hughes Hall to its new building, Shea–O'Brien Hall, named for Arthur V. Shea, S.J., and Eugene J. O'Brien, S.J.

1972   A thirteen-story residence is opened on East 191st Street. Known first as 555, it will later be renamed Walsh Hall, after Michael P. Walsh, S.J., President from 1969 to 1972.

1973   The inception of women's tennis.

1974   First Archbishop Hughes medals awarded to administrators for twenty years of service.

1975   Graduate School of Religion and Religious Education is developed out of the religious education programs begun in 1969.

1976   Vincent T. Lombardi Memorial Center is built and named in honor of alumnus, trustee, and professional football Hall of Fame Coach.

1976   Graduate Center on the campus of Marymount College in Tarrytown opens, with courses offered in business administration, education, and social service.

1977   Hispanic Research Center is established by its first and current director, Lloyd H. Rogler, Schweitzer Professor of Humanities.

1978   All-University Center on Gerontology is established with Brookdale Professor Marjorie H. Cantor. Msgr. Charles J. Fahey, Marie Ward Doty Professor, and director since 1979, presides over inception of doctoral program in Gerontology and a change of name to The Third Age Center.

1978   Fordham Hospital property (4.3 acres) purchased at auction from the City of New York for $400,000.

1979	Law School student team wins National Moot Court Competition.
1981	Alumni House is designated as Landmark Building by Landmarks Preservation Commission.
1982	First 1841 Awards presented to Physical Plant and clerical staff for twenty years of service.
1986	Completion of Rosehill Apartments, a Fordham-sponsored, federally subsidized residence for senior citizens and the handicapped, on a strip of abandoned park land adjacent to Fordham Prep.
1986	Sesquicentennial Residence Hall built.
1987	Alumni Court Residence Hall built.
1990	September 30. Sesquicentennial year, with the theme "Keeping Faith with the Future," opens with Mass of the Holy Spirit and Convocation.
1990	October 2. New Hall renamed Finlay Hall after James C. Finlay, s.j., President from 1972 to 1984.